Frank Hulin

The Pater

He prayeth best, who loveth best,
All things both great and small;
For the dear God who loveth us,
He made and loveth all.

Thou shalt save both man and beast.

Birds are the living praises of God.

FRONTISPIECE — Bas-relief moulded by John Lockwood Kipling (*courtesy of Misses Helen and Betty Macdonald*)

The Pater

John Lockwood Kipling
His Life and Times
1837-1911

by

Arthur R. Ankers

Pond View Books
Otford

First published in Great Britain 1988 by
Hawthorns Publications Limited,
Pond View House, Otford, Kent.

© Hawthorns Publications Limited 1988

ISBN 1 871044 00 6

Printed in Great Britain by
Unwin Brothers Limited
The Gresham Press
Old Woking
Surrey

CONTENTS

LIST OF ILLUSTRATIONS

FRONTISPIECE — Bas-relief moulded by John Lockwood Kipling
(courtesy of Misses Helen and Betty Macdonald)

ACKNOWLEDGEMENTS

The author is indebted to many people who, through the years, have provided help and encouragement.

These include the late A.W. Baldwin, Earl Baldwin of Bewdley; Mrs Louie Abbey (and her sister, Mrs Rawling): Messrs R.H. Blackburn, W. James Craig, Michael W. Hansell, John Mason (Archive Department, Thomas Cook Limited); David A. Miller, MA., (Head of Woodhouse Grove School and for permission to quote the late Dr F.C. Pritchard's *Story of Woodhouse Grove School*).

I am further indebted to John Shearman, former Secretary of the Kipling Society; John McGivering, member of the Council, Mrs G.H. Newsom, Kipling Society Librarian.

Much of the material embodied here is to be found in the Kipling Archive at the University of Sussex Library and is published by kind permission of the National Trust. I am especially in debt to John Burt who has charge of the Archive and to members of the Library staff for their unfailing patience and courtesy. Quotations from *Something of Myself* by Rudyard Kipling are by permission of A.P. Watt Limited, on behalf of the National Trust and Macmillan London Ltd. Permission to quote from *A Pilgrimage of Passion* by Lady Elizabeth Longford was granted by Messrs George Weidenfeld and Nicolson Ltd. Permission to quote from C.J. Davey's *Man for All Children* was graciously given by the author and the Epworth Press. Quotations from *Plain Tales from the Hills* and *Kim* came from Macmillan's Pocket Edition and from *Life's Handicap* and *The Light that Failed* came from Macmillan's First Editions.

My indebtedness extends to the Oxford University Press for permission to reprint part of *The Song of an Outsider* from *Early Verses* by Rudyard Kipling 1879-1889, edited by Andrew Rutherford.

I am very grateful to the Misses Helen and Betty Macdonald for the photographs of John Lockwood Kipling's family and original drawings by John Lockwood Kipling - 'The Snake Woman' and 'The Ruby Prince' and to The University of Sussex Library for John Lockwood Kipling drawings; also to The Kipling Society for permission to use a photograph of Alice Lockwood Kipling. I am also indebted to Worthing Central Library who obtained many out of print works for the author; to Professor Thomas Pinney who read my original manuscript and my grateful appreciation is extended to Mrs Margaret Littlewood who typed and re-typed my manuscript with unfailing patience and generosity. Should there be any whom I have overlooked but who, through the years, have been sources of help and encouragement, I offer my sincere thanks.

Arthur R. Ankers

JOHN KIPLING
(1730–1792)
m ANN (?)
   (1726–1808)

JOHN   (Eldest of two children)
(1773–1835)
m ANN HANSELL 1801   (Eldest of three daughters of
   (1782–1855)   Robert Hansell (1732–1795) and Alice, (nee
                       Harrison) (1746–1836) his second wife)

JOSEPH   (Eldest of seven children - three sons and four daughters)
(1805–1862)
m FRANCES LOCKWOOD 1836   Youngest of ten children – seven
   (1804–1886)   daughters and three sons – of William
                       Lockwood (1761–1829) (son of Joshua
                       (1717–?) and Dorothy, and grandson of
                       John Lockwood (late seventeenth
                       century–1735)) – m Ruth Merry, daughter
                       of Peter Merry (or Murray) (nee Oxley).
                       Also granddaughter of William Merry

JOHN (LOCKWOOD)   (Eldest of six children – two sons and four
(1837–1911)   daughters)
m ALICE MACDONALD 1865   Eldest surviving daughter – five girls and
   (1837–1910)   two sons
                       of George Browne Macdonald
                       (1805–1868) and Hannah (nee Jones)
                       (1809–1875)

JOSEPH RUDYARD   ALICE (Trix)
(1865–1936)   (1868–1948)
m CAROLINE STARR   m JOHN MURCHISON FLEMING
   BALESTIER 1892   1889
   (1862–1939)   (1858–1942)
                       (no issue)

JOSEPHINE   ELSIE   JOHN
(1892–1899)   (1896–1978)   (1897–1915)
             m George Bambridge d (1943)   (no issue)
             (no issue)

PREFACE

Some men have suffered the disadvantage of being born the sons of famous fathers; others that of having fathered famous sons: such a man was John Lockwood Kipling.

One of the results of this over-shadowing has been that his life and work have received less attention than they deserve.

Few fathers have stood in such a close and extended relationship as that enjoyed by John Lockwood Kipling and his son. On Rudyard's own confession they worked together for thirty years, during which time 'the Pater' was his literary mentor and, with his mother, constituted the only critics to whom he gave serious attention. For this reason, light shed on the father might well shed further light on the son.

That Rudyard Kipling was a complex character has been amply demonstrated by the numerous and erudite studies which have been made of him during recent years. Not only was he the child of a Celtic mother; he was also the son of a Yorkshire father. The mother was all 'celtic fire'; the father sage, sensible, imperturbable and always kind. That such a union should produce a son who became both poet and pioneer motorist, mystic and man of the world, puritan and sceptic, lover of dogs and children and hater of tourists and cant is scarcely surprising.

One of Rudyard's characteristics consisted of a deep-seated reticence regarding his private life. Private letters were destroyed and references to himself in other people's books were denied to their authors, (*Life of Jameson* - Ian Colvin). The same reticence may well account for the Pater's failure to continue his recollections of his early life beyond the age of seven and the formative years of his boyhood and adolescence are not recorded.

Fortunately, impelled partly by an inbred 'twist for writing', and partly by the pinch of poverty, in 1870 John Lockwood Kipling began a series of weekly contributions to an Indian journal the *Pioneer Mail*. It is through these columns that we are able to view events through the eyes of a perceptive Anglo-Indian. We are also given, not only a picture of the British Raj at the height of its power, but an insight into the mind and character of the writer.

Other sources of information regarding John Lockwood Kipling are to be found in a small collection of letters and memorabilia lodged with the University of Sussex Library.

Yorkshire - Mine Own Country

When asked in 1896 if he had Yorkshire blood in his veins, John Lockwood Kipling's son Rudyard replied: 'I believe that in a humble way few stocks carry back cleaner Yorkshire blood for a longer time. I think we are West Riding for a matter of two hundred years, a thing of which I am not a little proud.' Rudyard concluded his reply to a letter addressed to him by Dr Vaughan Bateson, the Bradford Police Surgeon; 'You may say fairly that I have a good claim to be called a Yorkshireman and, as a fellow tyke, I thank you once more for your kind expression of interest.'[1]

Despite this pride in his Yorkshire ancestry, Rudyard never seemed to discover exactly where in Yorkshire his family roots were to be found. Quite late in life he mentioned Snaith as a possible place of origin:[2] he was wrong, although his grandparents, the Revd Joseph and Mrs Kipling, had lived there for three years during which time Rudyard's father was away at school. So far as Skipton-in-Craven (the town mentioned in his letter to Dr Vaughan Bateson) is concerned, Rudyard could hardly have been more wide of the mark: just about the whole breadth of 'the county of broad acres' lay between Skipton and land of his more immediate ancestors, high up in the North Yorkshire moors - unless he had his Lockwood forebears in mind.

Although Rudyard boasted of being a Yorkshireman and 'a fellow tyke' and, on a number of occasions, thought nostalgically of Yorkshire as 'mine own country', he wrote about it more as a district to pass through rather than one in which he ever spent some length of time.

In the year 1921 he was driven in his Rolls-Royce (he never drove himself) along what was always known as the Great North Road. His intention was to reach the west coast of Scotland in easy stages. They cruised along (what Rudyard described as 'a perfect rubber-like road') at a steady forty miles an hour 'so that nobody passed us'.[3] As they picnicked by the road-side near Stamford he noted 'a steady stream of traffic' which passed by at the rate of one vehicle every minute!

After spending the Saturday night in Stamford they pressed on northwards until they reached Doncaster, 'empty in her Sabbath calm'. Still heading north they came to Harrogate, 'busy with Sunday motorists including lots of "wife-killers"'. On arrival at Ripon, they visited the cathedral which reminded them of Rouen Cathedral so that they were saddened by memories of former days when their dead son John used to navigate for them (and lose them too!) His father found consolation in hearing 'the good, meaty Yorkshire tongue again'.

Still heading northwards they lost their way near Brompton-on-Swale;

1

1. Briar Cottage, Lythe, North Yorkshire *(where the Revd Joseph Kipling was born — now called Kipling Cottage)*

2. Great Edstone Farm *(where the Revd Joseph Kipling grew up and from where he entered the Wesleyan Ministry)*

then, having extricated themselves they spent forty minutes trailing behind Bostock and Wombwell's menagerie, en route for Brough Horse-Fair.

They had now entered 'Kipling Country'. Across the River Swale from Catterick village lay the tiny hamlet of Kiplin with its magnificent Jacobean Hall originally built by George Calvert, a statesman in the time of James I, who became Lord Baltimore. During the course of his correspondence with F.H. Sunderland, Rudyard had been told that 'there was no doubt his family originated in Kipling, (*sic*) North Yorkshire, six miles north-west of Northallerton' and that they took their name from that small, picturesque village. He was misinformed.

Yet, unknown to Rudyard, he had now entered the country of his distant forebears. Not far away at the head of the valley of the River Swale lay the parish of Angram whose list of tenements for the year 1608 included the names of John and Thomas Kipling.[4]

As they drove over the fells, in the direction of Penrith, they passed through Bowes where at the end of the seventeenth century William Kipling, a cattle-dealer and 'gentleman', sent his son to Bowes Grammar School and thence to Worcester College, Oxford. There he graduated, was ordained and eventually became the Right Reverend Thomas Kipling, DD., Dean of Peterborough Cathedral. Not far from Bowes, at Romaldkirk, another John Kipling was baptized in the year 1579 and the name occurs frequently in the parish registers of Richmond, Bedale, Barnard Castle and Kirby Lonsdale. Some of the family were described as 'yeoman'; others graduated to the description of 'gentleman'.

The name, spelt in a variety of ways, goes back to the years which preceded the Domesday Book for, like so many of the words which abound in that part of England to this day (words such as dale, thwaite, sett, seat heath, ling, beck rigg, crag), the name 'Kipling' was originally of Norse extraction.

This proliferation of Norse names in the Pennine valleys came about through one of the many Viking invasions, which followed the Outer Line and landed in Ireland: there they founded the present city of Dublin. They then proceeded to make the Irish Sea a Scandinavian Lake and at the commencement of the tenth century AD, they descended on the north-western coasts of England and established their colonies in Lancashire and Cumbria; with the passage of time, they penetrated the Pennine valleys where they established their farms and turned the fells into sheep-runs.[5]

During the eighteenth century members of the Kipling family moved across the county of Yorkshire and found work on the farms of the Wolds and on the moors north of Whitby. It is there, in the village of Lythe, that John Lockwood Kipling's more immediate ancestors are to be found.

John Lockwood's grandfather (also named John) was employed by Robert Hansell who farmed a small-holding near Ugthorpe close to Lythe. He married Ann Hansell, the daughter of his employer, and for a time they lived in Briar Cottage (sometimes called Rose Cottage) in Lythe village. A subsequent occupant of that cottage, Mr Nelson Rawling, used to show visitors a 'wall-bed' in which he claimed that Lockwood Kipling's father, Joseph, was born as was also his brother, John. How John Lockwood would have rejoiced to hear of the local woman who refused to enter hospital saying, 'I were tupped i' this bed; I were lambed in it and I will die in it too!'

John Lockwood's grandmother, Ann, was described by an old Whitby fisherman as 'an old-fashioned puritan saint with a heart full of charity,' but who would 'never coat a disagreeable truth with sugar to suit the taste of a hypocrite.'

During the years they lived in Lythe, John and Ann became associated with the local Methodist Society as it used to be called. The family tradition has it that in 1759 the two cousins, John Kipling and Luke Hansell, crossed the moors to hear John Wesley preach in Guisborough; on their return they associated with others who, like them, had been influenced by the Methodist Revival. When it appeared that the Methodists were being ill-treated by both squire and parson, the Kiplings opened their cottage-home as a meeting-place: this led to John being taunted by some of his neighbours for having 'turned Methody' to which accusation he replied: 'Nay, but they be vastly better folk than you an' me!' However, he did 'turn Methody' and saw the two cottages, which had been turned into a place of worship, replaced by a chapel.

From their founder the early Methodists had inherited 'a passion for learning' and when their day's work was done, Joseph and his brother John used to walk into Whitby in order to borrow books from the recently founded Literary and Philosophical Society; thus they prepared the way for Joseph to enter the Wesleyan ministry and John to become a lay preacher. John also developed what was called 'a talent for versifying' of which the only example extant seems to be in the form of an acrostic poem on the name of his niece, Florence Rawling, which ran:-

> From every ill may the Lord protect,
> Long as your life shall last;
> On you may his favour and blessing descend,
> Receiving your thanks for the Past;
> Enrich your heart by His grace and love
> Nor leave you to wander wide,
> Cast round you His shield of strength from above
> Ever having the Lord for your Guide.

As a lay-preacher, John Kipling displayed a remarkable eloquence. According to R.T. Gaskin, the Whitby historian, who knew him personally, words poured from him in such a torrent that his hearers had difficulty in keeping up with his train of thought. He lived to old age and retired to the village of Sleights, near Whitby, where Rudyard's sister, Trix (Mrs Fleming), came to visit him.

Whilst this John Kipling seems to have been the extrovert of the family, his brother Joseph was of an introspective and reflective nature, a

4

characteristic which appeared at an early age. It was his mother's practice to attend the weekly class-meeting, one of the Methodist groups formed by John Wesley as a means whereby the spiritual and religious education of his converts might be fostered. A layman, or woman, known as the 'class-leader', encouraged the members to give an account of 'how the Lord had dealt with them during the past week; what temptations they had encountered and how they had overcome them' - a kind of group confessional.

One night Joseph went with his mother to her class-meeting and, for some reason - possibly because he deemed the boy too young to have had a religious experience - the class leader passed over Joseph without asking him the usual questions. When the boy reached home, he asked his mother what would happen to him if God were to pass him by. There is no record of Ann Kipling's reply, but her son grew up to become a local preacher and, much against his father's wishes, believed he had been called to the 'full-time' ministry!

His father's opposition is understandable, for the departure of his elder son, now twenty six years old, meant the loss to the family farm (now at Great Edstone near Kirbymoorside) of a pair of hands when farming was 'labour-intensive'. But the mother's will prevailed for, like Hannah of old, she had been glad to 'dedicate the first-fruit of her body to the service of God.'[7] This was the baby who was to become the father of John Lockwood Kipling and the grandfather of Rudyard: he was baptized Joseph.

Joseph Kipling's entry into the Wesleyan ministry was still further complicated by the fact that not only had he fallen in love with a lady who was one year his senior but, in accordance with rules of his church, marriage must be postponed for the several years he would be on probation.

The lady in question was Frances Lockwood, daughter of a builder and architect from Skelton-in-Cleveland on the northern fringe of the Whitby Moors. Frances' mother, Ruth, was the daughter of another architect, Peter Merry, and grand-daughter of William Merry, one of Lord Mulgrave's stewards in the estate office close to Lythe. It was he who featured in David Wilkie's painting, *Distraining for Rent*. On 6 September 1836, in Skelton-in-Cleveland Parish Church, Joseph and Frances 'plighted their troth' in the presence of the Vicar, the Revd W. Close. There was nothing strange about this proceeding for it was still customary for Methodists to marry according to the rites of the Church of England.

The home in Pickering to which Joseph took his bride was, according to their friend, Mary Benson,[8] little better than a cottage but Frances took with her household linen of her own spinning and was content to make the best of the furniture, which the local Methodists had thought fit to provide. Nor did she forget 'the purpose for which marriage was ordained' and a month after her wedding-day found herself pregnant. On 6 July 1837 she gave birth to a son who was registered under the Births and Deaths Registration Act of 1836 as 'John Kipling': it was many years before he added his mother's surname to his own and became known as John Lockwood Kipling.

At The Conference of 1823 the Methodists had issued a directive to its ministers regarding the choosing of a wife: it ran 'the marriage with a female not connected with our Society would be an instance of culpable imprudence, perilous to the preacher and likely to be injurious to the spiritual interests of our people.' So far as Joseph Kipling was concerned there was no cause for anxiety; it is certain he would never have shown himself a disobedient son of his church. Moreover, his choice of a bride certainly proved to be a wise one for Frances, with her commonsense, charm and sense of humour, was to show herself eminently fitted for the task of being a true 'help-meet' to her husband and an ornament to the church which she so deeply loved and so faithfully served.

The man Frances married was pale-faced, dark-eyed and stockily built with 'a voice of rare sweetness'. In his story, *On Greenhow Hill*, Rudyard Kipling has given us a picture of his grandfather in the shape of the hero of the story, the little minister, Amos Barraclough, 'wi a voice that would charm a bird offen a bush.'[9] The large-hearted charity which led to his befriending the somewhat uncouth John Learoyd (not to mention his dog, Blast) was typical of the Revd Joseph Kipling.

By nature he was shy and retiring and public life must have proved something of a trial to him. Mrs Fleming, his grand-daughter, used to say that he was a poor preacher[10] but, in a county where sermon-tasting was a popular recreation, Joseph earned the reputation of being 'a preacher of picturesque and dramatic power' whose sermons were orderly in construction, clear and Biblically-based. His sermon entitled 'The Eternal Nature of Hell's Torments' was (not surprisingly) long remembered, especially as it was delivered by so gentle and kindly a man: only a deep concern for the immortal souls of his people could have prompted it.

Joseph was received into the ranks of the ministry several years before the opening of the first Wesleyan Theological Seminary. For this reason he received no formal training in divinity: this does not mean that he had no professional training for, during the five years of his probation, he would be required to study set-books under the direction of his Superintendent.

One of the most remarkable examples of what autodidacticism can accomplish was demonstrated by one of his contemporaries, James Macdonald, (Rudyard's great-grandfather, distaff side) who, with little or no assistance from others, became a good Latin scholar and learned enough Greek and Hebrew to be able to read the scriptures in the original tongues: he also acquired an excellent knowledge of French and could read Italian, Spanish and Portuguese.[11] Such erudition must have put many a formally-educated clergyman to shame. Books were his chief delight and it is not surprising that for years he was assistant editor of the *Methodist Magazine*. Although it was never suggested that Joseph attained such academic heights, it is quite apparent that his son, John, recognised that his father was no fool: he always kept a photograph of him in his study and when Editha Plowden sought for a photograph of 'John Kipling's father' she described him as 'the learned Methodist Minister', a description she could only have received from 'her kindest friend', John Lockwood Kipling.[12]

So far as physique was concerned, Joseph Kipling was short in stature with sturdy legs developed by generations of hill-country farmers. This characteristic he passed on to his son and grandson and when John came to write his 'romance in two chapters', *Inezilla*, he described trousers as 'the invention of a spindle-shanked man in an attempt to hide the sharpness of his shins.'

In her younger days Frances, Joseph's wife, was 'a dark-eyed brunette' and Rudyard resembled her. He had the same thick eye-brows inherited from the Merry side of Frances' family. Frances' children alternated between apple-blossom blondes and Spanish brunettes, her first born son John (Lockwood) being one of the former and, in his early days distinguished by his golden beard.

It was Frances' practice to rise every morning at six o'clock and to nourish her soul on the Bible and prayer. She called Sunday her 'festival day' and treasured its hours 'as a miser his gold'. Her undoubted piety was touched with the saving grace of humour which ran like a golden thread through her whole life. Even when she lay dying it refused to desert her. Invited by her nurse to take her medicine she replied with a smile, 'Barkis is willun!' The novels of Charles Dickens had long been the delight of the Kipling family and when John, living in Bombay, learned of the writer's death, he wrote in the *Pioneer*: 'For thirty years many out here have laughed and wept, as he chose they should, over his inimitable mirth and irresistible pathos and, in dull up-country stations and dreary travellers' bungalows, have beguiled weary days and tedious nights with his books, the first reading of which is remembered always as a period to look back upon regretfully as among those delights in life that only come once.'[13]

Near the end of her life the doctor took hold of Frances' wrist to see if a faint pulse remained and when he asked 'Whose hand am I touching?', Frances opened her eyes and replied, 'The hand of youth and beauty!': the last thing to disappear from that face, 'chaste as an old cameo', was the smile.

During the course of their married life Frances bore her husband eight children, all but two of whom lived to old age; an excellent record for the time. Two boys, still-born, were the last she conceived and by then she was in her mid-forties.

The rearing of a family, consisting of two boys and four girls, without falling into debt, involved strict economies on the part of Joseph and Frances and their 'life-style', at all times, called for 'plain living' as well as 'high thinking'.

Then no London newspaper cost less than fivepence, the modern equivalent being a pound. John Wesley used to say that he read the newspapers in order to see what God was doing in His world and it seems that Joseph Kipling wished to do the same: his problem was how to afford it. The report of the

Poor Law Commissioners for 1834 had described the price of a newspaper as 'an insurmountable obstacle to the education of the poor' and whilst the lot of the Kiplings could not be compared with that of the town and country labourer they were always strangers to anything approaching affluence.

As a result the Revd Joseph developed the habit of snatching a glance at the newspapers which the better-off members of his flock could afford, an exercise in which he used to engage whilst on his pastoral rounds. According to the family traditions, the day came when he was caught 'red-handed' whilst engaged in this particular ploy. He had immersed himself in *The Times* when Frances heard their host approaching. She snatched away the newspaper and sat on it but when the owner asked if Mr Kipling had read Mr Bright's recent speech in the House and *The Times* could not be found, a blushing Mrs Kipling was forced to admit she was sitting on it![14]

Other economies were made through Joseph's skill as a gardener and the cultivation of his vegetable plot. After his profession, his two great loves were music and nature. As a naturalist he was accustomed to record his observations with great accuracy and in a beautiful and artistic hand: as a gardener it was his practice to carry out a daily tour of inspection of his crops.

It was during the course of one of these inspections that Joseph noticed that a branch had been broken off his favourite cherry tree: not only had the branch been thrown over the garden wall but the culprit had attempted to hide his 'crime' by smearing mud over the resulting gash. When challenged the children would not take refuge in a lie but confessed their guilt and had enough confidence in their father to ask how they had been found out. Instead of receiving the castigations normally handed out to naughty children, their father gave them a talk on 'the importance of little things' and revealed that one of the clues leading to the detection of their crime was a dislodged piece of moss from the wall. It was this power of observation which made him a fine naturalist and was to make his son John, the artist and descriptive writer he became.

A hundred years ago a Methodist minister was not expected to remain more than two or three years in the same town. This 'annual shuffle of the Methodists', as it became known, meant that after two years in Pickering, where John had been born, the family moved to Horncastle. They remained there for three years during which time Frances bore another boy, Joseph, and the first of her four girls, Jane Frances.

It was during their years in Horncastle that Susan Wilkinson was engaged as a servant; she was to remain with them for the next seventeen years. Her father was employed in a local boat-building yard and one of John's earliest recollections was of being taken there to witness the launching of a barge-boat.

From Horncastle the Kiplings moved to Howden, a busy market-town and the centre of a vast agricultural district. Here John was sent to his first school: it was kept by a Miss James, remembered by him in after-years as living in a pretty house close to the famous Minster and possessing two rosy cheeks and a red wig.

At one time Howden was famous for its annual Horse-Fair, referred to by Charles Dickens[15] but, because the Fair attracted shady characters and there was the ever-present fear of children being abducted by gypsies, the Kipling children were not allowed out unattended during the Fair time. This restriction led to John being taunted by his school-mates because he 'didn't dare', so Joseph determined that he himself would take his small son to see 'the fun of the fair'.

John was then about six years of age and one event he witnessed that day remained in his memory for more than sixty years. It seems that a gypsy-man tried to sell his father a cob; to make the animal hold its tail up and look sprightly, the vendor had pushed a piece of ginger inside its 'back passage'. As the horse was trotted up and down the ginger fell out and, before young John's astonished eyes, the gypsy picked it up, popped it in his mouth for a moment and then re-inserted it inside the cob.[16]

After attending Miss James' school, John was transferred to one kept by a Mr Hawkins: it overlooked a farm-yard and years later he recalled the fearful fascination with which he and his friends watched as a colt was thrown on a pile of straw and gelded.

While at Howden one of his friends was Sam Kemp, son of a local farmer, and when Sam was sent to count his father's cattle he rode on a donkey, sometimes with John Kipling riding behind. The local Sunday School Superintendent, obviously a kindly man, observed one Sunday that the boys could do something he could not do: it proved to be 'riding on a donkey'. Young John despised him as 'a duffer' and so began his life-long disenchantment with religious folk!

Another of his early recollections concerned a cow which had 'horned' the son of its owner because he interfered with her calf. When a neighbour sympathised with the lad's misfortune and accused the cow of 'abominable behaviour', the farmer disagreed. 'Why no ma'am,' he said, 'the cow were in her dooty for we must all purtect our young.'[17]

There was also the local blacksmith's account of how he once 'shoed a bull'. This must have been a spectacular proceeding because the animal had first to be thrown so that its legs could be fixed to a framework to enable the smith to fit two pieces of metal to each of its cloved hooves. Years afterwards John wrote: 'I silently marvelled, after the fashion of children, how the feat was done for the bull I knew most intimately was a fearsome beast, safe to stroke in his stall but awful in field or garth.'[18]

This interest in animals and his understanding of them was to re-appear in John's son, Rudyard, and to inspire some of his best-known stories.

During Joseph's ministry in Howden his ministerial colleague was an elderly man, the Revd Charles Radcliffe. He had a son, Charles Bland Radcliffe, a medical student at the University of Paris. It was whilst the young man was home on vacation that young John Kipling damaged the end

9

of one of his fingers in the handle of their pump. Susan, the maid-servant, who must have seen many such mishaps in the boat-yard where her father worked, was inclined to make light of the injury, but when the Revd Joseph saw it he was incensed. Turning on the unfortunate girl he exclaimed, 'You don't care what the devil becomes of the lad's finger', an explosion of wrath which made John marvel, for such strong language had never been heard in the Kipling home. It was young Mr Radcliffe who came to the rescue, glad no doubt of an opportunity to practise his newly acquired skills. He expertly dressed the injured finger and bound it up, thereby possibly saving a future craftsman from disablement![19]

Years later Charles Bland Radcliffe had his own consulting rooms in Henrietta Street, Cavendish Square, and was the family doctor to John Kipling's sister-in-law, Georgiana Burne-Jones and her husband Edward - an associate of the brotherhood of painters, the pre-Raphaelites. In her *Memorials of Edward Burne-Jones* she paid tribute to two occasions on which she and her family became deeply indebted to the same Dr Radcliffe.

The first occasion fell on Christmas Eve, 1861: her husband had gone early to bed and was overtaken by a bout of coughing which brought on a haemorrhage. Georgie rushed out into the street, caught a cab (it was before the day of the telephone) and drove to Henrietta Street. Dr Radcliffe had hoped to be free on that one particular night 'from the haunting calls of his profession' but when Georgie showed him the handkerchief with its terrible crimson stains, he at once returned with her to the house in Kensington Square, bringing with him 'his never-failing steadiness and help'. Fortunately the blood came from the throat, and not from the lungs, and the problem never recurred.[20]

Only a year later Georgie's son, Philip, developed congestion of the lungs and once more the physician, who was also their friend, came to the rescue. 'All one afternoon,' wrote Georgie, 'there was a fight with death which the doctor won!'[21] By way of a thank-offering, Edward Burne-Jones gave Dr Radcliffe a drawing entitled 'The Mother of Healing': it depicted the Virgin Mary with the Christ-Child on her knee whilst in the background lay a sick child in bed - Philip. At the feet of the Virgin the same child, now recovered, played happily.

That child grew up to become, like his father, an artist and a close friend of his cousin Rudyard whose portrait, now in the National Portrait Gallery, he was to paint. He also painted Rudyard's wife, Carrie, and her portrait hangs over the fire-place in his study at Bateman's. It was a far-cry from the Methodist manse in Howden to the elegance of Kensington Square, yet the young medical student, who may well have saved the hand of a future architectural sculptor, was to become the physician who saved the life of the painter of what is the best known portrait of John Kipling's famous son.

In the late summer of 1844 the Revd Joseph Kipling, accompanied by his wife, his two sons and three daughters, left Howden for their new home in Bridlington. They commenced their journey by travelling in the horse-bus which plied between Howden and Hull. There they changed conveyances not far from the statue of one of Hull's most famous sons, William Wilberforce, 'the great abolitionist'.

The next year, within a few weeks of his eighth birthday and 'a timorous child', young John set out for the Wesleyan Academy for the sons of the Ministry at Apperley Bridge, near Bradford. Looking back, he believed he was sent from home while still too young yet, quite inconsistently, he sent his own son away before he was six, accompanied by his little sister, then only three! Admittedly, the circumstances were different: the climate of breezy Bridlington was rather more salubrious than that of Bombay!

References Chapter One

1. Holograph in possession of the Author
2. KA 17/35
3. KA 25,7 and 8
4. *Muker - a Yorkshire Parish* - E.Cooper
5. *The Pennine Dales* - A. Raistrick
4. Revd Sam Davies to Author
7. l.Sam.1,xi
8. KA 20/1
9. *On Greenhow Hill* p.27
10. KA 3/19
11. Letters of James Macdonald
12. Letters in possession of Author
13. *Pioneer Mail* 13.6.1871
14. KA 15/2
15. *Bentley's Review*
16. KA 3/16
17. *Beast and Man in India* p.122
18. *Beast and Man in India* p.238
19. KA 3/16
20. *Memorials of Edward Burne-Jones* p.234
21. *Memorials of Edward Burne-Jones* p.238

3. Woodhouse Grove School *(from an engraving in the Illustrated London News, September 1882)*

Apperley Bridge - A Dreary Methodist School

'A dreary Methodist School' - it was in these terms that John Kipling's daughter Trix described Woodhouse Grove, the school established in 1812 by the Methodist Church for the education of the sons of its ministers.[1] The only comments made by her father about his school still extant, are to the effect that he left home when far too young and was 'a timorous child'. It is a pity that the recollections of early life, made in his closing years, ceased with the move from Howden in East Yorkshire to Bridlington. His memories of those critical years during which he attended the Woodhouse Grove Academy (as it was then known) would have been most illuminating.

Fortunately, the recollections of other old boys, some of whom were contemporary with John, were collected and published in 1885 by Josiah Thomas Slugg, FRAS under the title, *Woodhouse Grove School: Memorials and Reminiscences*. Ninety years later, Frank Cyril Pritchard, a former Headmaster of the Grove, wrote *The Story of Woodhouse Grove School*, a comprehensive and well-documented account of the school's history based mainly on extant official records and, in particular, on the Minutes of the Committee of Management.

Before being bought by the Methodist Connexion, Woodhouse Grove had been advertised in the *Morning Chronicle* as 'an elegant mansion house adapted for the residence of a large genteel family.' It consisted, so the advertisement continued, of 'drawing and dining rooms of large dimensions with breakfast room, study, butler's pantry, house-keeper's room, servants hall, kitchens and every other convenience on the ground floor; twelve lodging rooms, dressing room and accommodation for servants, wash-house, laundry, brew-house and other offices.' There were out-buildings consisting of stabling for twelve horses, a double coach-house and harness room. Conveniently detached was a farm-yard with a large barn, cow-house and pigging-house. All the buildings were in free-stone and in good repair. The gardens contained about seven acres and in front of the house lay a further eight acres 'ornamented with large oaks and other fine timbers'.[2] Water was supplied by a 'never-failing spring of soft water'. For miles around, the countryside abounded in game 'and was ornamented with the seats of many families of distinction'. The mansion stood on the slopes of the Vale of Apperley with the River Aire, then unpolluted, running in the bottom and separating the school from Calverley Wood on the opposite side of the valley. The nearest town was Bradford, four miles away across open fields and moorland, thus fulfilling John Wesley's dictum that a Methodist school should be 'not too far from a town which would be highly inconvenient for a large family: nor yet too near... which would have been attended with greater evils'[3]; presumably those threatening the moral health of the scholars!

With their remarkable aptitude for recognising a good site when they saw it (witness their purchase at a later date of the site for the Westminster Central Hall, opposite to the Abbey, as their headquarters), the Methodists bought the Grove for £4,575, described at the time as the largest pecuniary enterprise into which they had ever entered.

When they indulged in this extraordinary 'pecuniary enterprise' the Methodist concern was to build a northern equivalent to John Wesley's foundation near Bristol, Kingswood School, built especially for the sons of Wesley's preachers. Both Kingswood and Woodhouse Grove offered six years free schooling for the sons of the manse for eleven months of the year. They also provided clothes and shoes, thus relieving the ministers' families, often large, of a considerable financial burden. There was, however, one qualification: no minister was allowed to enter his son who had not subscribed five guineas towards the paying-off of the debt on the school. A concession was later offered by which any deficiencies could be made up by a series of easy payments over a period of years, thus introducing, perhaps for the first time, hire-purchase!

The aims of the new school were outlined in the sermon preached by the Revd James Wood, Chairman and Treasurer of the School Management Committee, 1811-14. They were 'to qualify boys to fill some useful station in civil life and to guard them from the corruption which frequently abounds in large numbers of giddy youths; to give them an acquaintance with the best things, yet, may it please God to call some of these to fill the places of their fathers in the Church of Christ, and to be instruments of good to the rising generation.'[4]

Twenty years later more modest aims were expressed in the 1830 Report to the Methodist Conference. 'It was not expected,' it ran, 'that individuals educated in our seminaries should attain to eminent and exalted stations but in all reasonable anticipation the great mass of our pupils are destined to a happier lot, to tread the paths of middle life and to amalgamate with those numerous and important sections of our populations whose general designation is that highly honourable one of the yeomanry of Britain.'[5] One thing was made plain; it was that the school did not set out to produce 'young gentlemen', a limitation which was made quite clear in 1835 when the Head's wife, Mrs Joshua Wood, advertised 'a Seminary for Young Ladies' to be opened in her official residence. The Committee of Management was quick to remind her that 'No school for young gentlemen or young ladies can be allowed in any circumstances on the premises of the Woodhouse Grove Institution.'[6] It seems that the sons of the Wesleyan ministry did not qualify for the title 'young gentlemen', only 'young yeomen.' Wesleyan Methodism was on its way to becoming a largely middle-class church.

Before pursuing the story of John Kipling's school it might be advisable to digress for a moment in order to compare it with another and similar school founded some twenty years after the opening of Woodhouse Grove - Marlborough College.

Like the Grove, Marlborough was established originally for the education of the sons of the Christian ministry, in this case, 'the lesser clergy': like the Grove it was based in a country mansion, The White House, Marlborough, to which was joined the Castle Inn and ten acres of grounds. The decline in coaching along the Great Bath Road and the advance of the railway systems accounted for the sale of it, with the result that stables and out-buildings became dormitories, masters' rooms and servants' accommodation.

Marlborough enjoyed two advantages denied to the boys at Woodhouse Grove who, in its early days, were subjected to a near-monastic regime: Marlborough allowed its pupils to wander abroad in the glorious countryside which surrounded it and permitted them to return home both at the end of the first half of the school year and again for the summer vacation. Woodhouse Grove only allowed its pupils to return home once a year.

The original idea was that Marlborough should, like the Grove, be exclusively for the sons of the clergy but this was soon abandoned, and admission granted to the sons of the laity. This enabled a partner in a firm of discount-brokers to send his son to the new school; the boy's name was William Morris who, in later years, became a friend of the Kipling family and known to Rudyard as 'Uncle Topsy' on account of his shaggy mass of hair. His judgement in later life on his old school was summed up in the words: 'I learned next to nothing for, indeed, next to nothing was taught me.' This was no doubt a piece of hyperbole, yet it stands in stark contrast to Morris's contemporary, John Kipling, who left Woodhouse Grove, not only with a solid foundation of knowledge but with a delight in learning, and an intellectual curiosity which never left him.

In its early days it was usual for the pupils to spend eleven months of each year at the Grove followed by four to five weeks for the summer vacation. This occurred 'around the month of May' and it was not until some years after John Kipling had left that a Christmas holiday was granted. The parents had to pay their son's travelling expenses except when a compulsory evacuation of the school, usually through a local outbreak of small-pox or cholera, became essential. On such occasions, where parents were unable to afford the cost of travel, or to maintain their children at home, the 'Children's Fund' would come to their aid.

Before the development of the railways, travel in England was often a long and tedious undertaking. In 1845 John Kipling would find himself more fortunately placed than some of his school-mates: he was able to take the train as far as Bradford and either walk or take some rural horse-bus four miles to Apperley Bridge. For some boys to reach school meant 'shank's pony' all the way; nor was this situation unusual. In 1820, when Rudyard's great-grandfather Macdonald sent instructions to his son, George, as to how he was to reach Todmorden from Apperley Bridge, he was directed to walk first to Halifax; there a local Wesleyan minister would lodge him for the night. The next forenoon he was to walk as far as Heptonstall and either lodge with Revd Mr Layton overnight, or borrow his pony and reach Todmorden in time for dinner. His father said that he would be ashamed if his son was to regard twelve, fifteen, or even twenty miles a day walk as a hardship.[7] At least one of the boys was accustomed to take a sailing-ship to Hull, a coach to Leeds and then presumably walk the rest of the way. Allowance was made for the difficulties of travel but if a pupil failed to materialise within a week he was expelled. As there was always a waiting list (not a surprising fact seeing that the education, board, clothes and even pocket money were all free), one may be sure that parents saw to it that their sons arrived on time. Some indeed ran away and for this the penalty was always expulsion. One cannot imagine that the culprit was warmly welcomed at home!

When John Kipling arrived at the Grove in 1844 it was expected that he would have brought with him (or on him) two suits, two pairs of shoes, six linen shirts and six pairs of stockings.These would be listed and when the time came for him to leave he would be supplied with their equivalent. The school, in the meantime, would supply him with a blue cloak, jacket and waist-coat, corderoy trousers, a leather cap (in the early days sealskin) and two pairs of shoes each year. In the event of the shoes being worn out within a year, the owner was condemned to go in clogs! The school also provided a tailor and a cobbler to make 'running-repairs'. The parents were expected to contribute four guineas (£4.20p) a year towards this outfit. For all the pupils the only opportunity they had of seeing their parents apart from the summer vacation, was when the Annual Conference of the Methodist Connexion met in either Leeds or Bradford. If held in Leeds, the journey from Apperley Bridge was made by barge along thirteen miles of the Leeds-Liverpool Canal; should it be in Bradford, a four miles walk across open country and moorland had to be faced. The only time that this privilege occurred for John Kipling was in 1850 when the Conference met in Leeds.

On arrival at the Grove, John would find himself one of about forty occupants of a small dormitory known as the 'crib-room' as the boys slept in wooden 'cribs'. Diseases like typhus, rheumatic fever, meningitis as well as the usual illnesses of childhood, were common. During Kipling's first year six boys died whilst at school! John himself was critically ill in 1846 and it was only John Wesley's dictum that 'cleanliness was akin to godliness' which probably saved his life. The value of good ventilation was realised and in the classrooms there was a ten minute 'ventilation break' during both the morning and afternoon sessions: the airing of the dormitories was also rigorously insisted upon.

Two years after Kipling's coming to his school a series of extensions were embarked on: these included the building of two airy and commodious dormitories, a new dining hall, a library and new kitchens. Concern was expressed regarding the proximity of the goods-yard of the local railway station to the new buildings for, in order to raise money, the school had sold part of the estate to the Midland Railway Company. It was feared that the conversations of railway workers and coal carriers might corrupt the boys' morals, so their sleeping accommodation was built as far as possible from the suspected source of infection.

At the same time tenders were invited for the installation of a coal-gas plant to replace the candles and oil lamps which, according to one of the staff, 'only made the darkness of the schoolroom visible'. When this came into production not only was the railway station supplied with gas but also several of the adjoining houses Only ten years earlier the Provost of Eton College had met a delegation who requested that tapped water should be laid on to the College. His retort was that 'they would be wanting gas-lighting and turkey carpets next'.[8]

An amusing by-product of the gas installation was an epic poem of thirty stanzas entitled 'The Downfall of Lamps and Candles and the Rise of Gas at Woodhouse Grove Academy.'[9]

John Kipling's entry into Woodhouse Grove took place during the 'Hungry Forties' so conditions were spartan. For five days a week breakfast and supper each consisted of a slice of dry bread and a mug of milk, the latter warmed (and diluted) in winter by the addition of hot water. On two days each week the menu consisted of porridge, treacle and water. Dinner was taken at midday and consisted of two courses, one of meat and vegetables and the other of pudding. Should the latter be of the Yorkshire variety it was eaten before the main course, in accord with local custom, thus taking the edge off youthful appetites! Generally speaking the food served was not lacking so much in quantity as in the manner in which it was served. Indeed, at one period the Governor used to come round after dinner looking for uneaten food which he called 'marginal references'; any boy found guilty was punished - hardly a common occurrence for, no doubt, if the boy himself proved unequal to the portions served him, his companions would be eager to help him out.

Classes recommenced at two in the afternoon and, apart from the usual 'ventilation break' of ten minutes, continued until five. Supper was served at 5.30 p.m. and 'prep' began at 6.30 p.m. Bedtime for the whole school came at 8 p.m., regardless of age but this was modified later, and the senior boys were allowed to stay up for an extra hour. Twenty years after John Kipling left the Grove, a Special Enquiry found that the boys got nothing in the way of food and drink between 5.30 p.m. and 8.30 the next morning and steps were taken to mitigate this rather cruel state of affairs.

Part of the school estate was devoted to agricultural purposes such as the grazing of cows and the growing of potatoes. In view of the rigours described, this crop was the subject of illicit raids culminating with the roasting of potatoes on the school furnace.

In common with the practice of public schools, the curriculum concentrated on the teaching of languages, mainly classical. The weekly time-table could include nine hours of Greek, nine of Latin and six of French. With the advent of Samuel Sharpe, MA, LLB., classics were not overlooked but such subjects as mathematics, practical chemistry and mechanics were introduced into the curriculum, an indication possibly of the expanding influence of the Industrial Revolution. These changes do not seem to have met with the approval of at least one Old Grovian for, in 1870, John Kipling wrote: 'English schoolboys were taught to praise the old Roman who knew how to die when necessary ... and to applaud the coolness with which Socrates accepted the hemlock from the Athenian Senate; at least they used to do in my time. Nowadays they learn book-keeping, chemistry and high-dutch!'[10]

The Committee of Management discovered in 1842 that the teaching of the Christian religion was being neglected and ordered that each Saturday morning should be devoted to the study of 'The Evidences, Doctrines and Duties of Christianity'.[11] Whatever neglect there had been, John Kipling emerged with a wide knowledge of the language of the King James Bible, quotations from which abound in his writings. Three attendances at the neighbouring Wesleyan Chapel each Sunday may well have had something to do with this.

It was some time before the growing public school obsession with organised games, such as football and cricket, affected Woodhouse Grove, one reason being that a considerable part of the estate was devoted to the pasturing of cattle and the cultivation of vegetables to supply the school dining-hall: thus there was no room for those games which required a lot of space.

In view of this it is scarcely surprising that John Kipling never showed much enthusiasm for organised sport and tended to view games, and those who participated in them, through the eyes of an amused and somewhat cynical observer. He did confess to the enjoyment of ice-skating and 'rinking' (roller-skating) but his motives seem to have lain more in the enjoyment of the female society with which these activities were associated, rather than with the love of the sport itself. As for 'the flannelled fools and muddied oafs' of Rudyard's verses, they rarely commanded his attention.

Unattractive examples of school-boys 'sport' found at Woodhouse Grove took the form of what can be called 'group-bullying': amusing perhaps to the spectators but painful for the victims, especially for boys of a sensitive nature.

One example of this horse-play was known at the Grove as 'belling'. The selected victim, chosen to provide amusement for his school-fellows, was forcibly seated at the top of a flight of seven stone steps: his legs were then seized by his tormentors and he was dragged to the bottom in a series of painful bumps.[12]

Bullying was by no means confined to Woodhouse Grove. A century earlier John Wesley had left the Charterhouse haunted by memories of the hounding, beating and half-starving of the smaller and weaker boys by the older and stronger. Thus, when he came to found his own school, Kingswood, he ruled that the pupils should be subject to constant supervision by the masters so as to prevent bullying. A similar rule was applied at the Grove but was only partially successful, with the result that the new boy soon discovered that the sons of the ministry were far from angelic by nature and was given a hard and tearful education in the ways of boys with each other.[13]

Nor were the sons of the Methodist parsons unique in this respect. Mention has been made of Marlborough College, founded for the sons of 'the lesser clergy' and attended by William Morris, a contemporary of John Kipling. It was only his remarkable strength which saved him from the cruelties which were inflicted on weaker boys and which included being suspended from the upstairs balconies of The White House or of being 'roasted' in front of the school-room fires which they were unable to get near, on account of the bigger lads, until it was their turn to provide sport.[14]

Could it be that one of the causes of the aversion which John Kipling came to display towards the church of his fathers was deep-rooted in the experiences of a shy and timorous child, torn from a gentle, kindly home-circle at too early an age, and subject to the cruelties which even the 'sons of the Manse' were capable of inflicting. William Morris claimed that his schooldays taught him one thing - rebellion, and they may well have influenced his rejection of Victorian taste in art as well as his rejection of the idea of becoming an Anglican clergyman. In similar fashion John Kipling was to emerge as a rebel against the religious concepts and practices in the midst of which he had been brought up; like Morris he sought fulfilment in the realm of art and craftsmanship.

The sadistic element in human nature found an out-let, not only in the treatment by boys of their school-mates but also in the school-masters' treatment of their pupils. The flogging of children ran like a dark stain through the fabric of Victorian righteousness: it was frequently alleged to be in fulfilment of the Biblical warning that 'to spare the rod was to spoil the child'; thus, backed by divine sanction, merciless flagellations were administered in the schools, both preparatory and public. The 'flogging Head' became quite a feature of Victorian school life. In John Kipling's school, the cane was the symbol of the pedagogue's authority and his main sanction. When a senior boy came to be appointed a 'pupil teacher' he was handed a cane, not only to be displayed as the symbol of his authority but as the means of enforcing it.[15] An 'Old Grovian' of 1856-61 vintage wrote of the school in his day: 'The fare was spartan, the discipline spartan; there was a cane on every table and all mistakes in declensions, principle parts and parsing involved six cuts on the hand and every afternoon before tea there was a general post-mortem in which all the offences of the day were dealt with; some had corporal punishment and were flogged; others had lines to write out, five hundred or thousand times.'[16] One of the more progressive masters, appointed after John had left, made it a habit to explain to the delinquent he was about to punish that he did so 'out of high regard for his father'. One is bound to speculate on the effect such an excuse had on family relationships!

John recalled that the Head used to beat him for what he described as 'stoical apathy', meaning perhaps a cocoon of indifference inside which this sensitive child was accustomed to hide himself.

Whether this obsession with corporal punishment sprang from a sincere zeal in the performance of duty, or a regard for the victim's parents, or from more sinister motives, must remain a matter of speculation but, so far as the Grove was concerned, it is only fair to add that the Committee of Management had issued a directive to the effect that 'no greater degree of severity should be used than is absolutely necessary'. Whether this was generally observed is another matter.

In order to keep the Grove situation in historical perspective it must be seen in comparison with other boarding schools of that era. Contemporary with John Kipling were Wilfrid Scawen Blunt and his brother Francis, who were sent to a preparatory school at Twyford, Hants. Blunt not only described the school as 'the most hideous epitome of the world's wickedness', but also recalled how he and his brother wandered on the Downs in search of scraps of food discarded by the race-goers.[17] And when on a cold grey day in January, 1878 Rudyard entered 'twelve bleak houses by the shore' at Westward Ho, he found the school 'primitive in its appointments' and was offered food which 'would have raised a mutiny in Dartmoor'.[18]

At the Grove the food was eaten from tin plates and the boys drank from tin mugs, a practice which continued until 1858 when two former pupils, by then partners in a firm of earthenware manufacturers at Burslem, Staffordshire, presented their 'alma mater' with two hundred and fifty china mugs decorated with a drawing of the school frontage underneath the glaze. They were partners in the Burslem firm of Pinder, Bourne and Company, one of whose designers was John Kipling. It would be interesting to know if it was he who suggested the gift or, more likely, whether he was responsible for the design.[19]

The school day began at 5.45 a.m. (6.45 in the winter), no doubt to economise on oil and candles. The rising bell was rung by the most junior master who then proceeded to the dormitories where he would give the command 'All rise!' Five minutes later came the second order 'All kneel!'; to be followed by the command 'Rise', after which the boys marched off to the lavatories and thence to the school for one hour's schooling in the winter and two hours in the summer. Prayers came at 8 a.m. and breakfast at 8.30 a.m. By 9 a.m. the boys were back in the class-room.

Sunday, as might be expected, was different. At 10.30 a.m., again at 3.00 p.m. and finally at 6.00 p.m., the school marched down the drive to chapel where they were able to view some of their village neighbours and where, at times, they were entertained by the performances in the pulpit of homely lay-preachers. Between the morning and afternoon services in chapel the younger boys had to learn their catechism, whilst the older pupils studied the Greek New Testament. After the evening service came supper consisting of a slice of bread and a mug of water. Little wonder that when 'he became a man' John Kipling had little appetite for the practice of public worship!

In the latter part of her life John's daughter, Trix, described the Grove as 'dreary'. Apart from any prejudice she felt this may have been the impression gained from her father, of the near-monastic conditions under which the boys lived. With a few exceptions they were confined to the school-room, the dining hall, the dormitory and a small play-ground. No boy was allowed outside the school bounds unless in the company of a master: some of these were lay-preachers and it was a privilege to go with one of these preachers to his appointment in some neighbouring village. It was said that one of the Headmasters was so stout that when he went out to preach he invariably took six boys with him to push him up the hills. To be condemned to pass eleven months of the year in such confinement could well incur the description of 'dreary'.

There were occasional exceptions to this rule, one of which occurred in the month of August. This took the form of a school picnic at Otley Chevin, high up on the moors which separate Airedale from Wharfedale. The small boys were taken in carts; the better-off hired donkeys for a shilling a day, whilst the rest walked the four or five miles to the top. The excuse for this reckless exhibition of levity was that it was in celebration of William Wilberforce, the great abolitionist, whose statue John had passed by in the 1844 journey to Bridlington.

In his contribution to the *Kipling Journal*, James Craig observes that the Grove was apparently 'run on a shoe-string'. It was, and this is hardly surprising when it is remembered that it was 'non-fee-paying' until 1883 when the sons of the laity were admitted. Its very existence depended on grants from church funds and thus on the generosity of the Wesleyan Methodist people. In spite of this situation, not only did the boys receive free tuition, board and lodging, but also their clothing and even pocket money. Although pocket money only amounted to three halfpence a week, from which one halfpenny was deducted 'For Missions', it was at least a gesture of good-will and might be subsidised by the boy's parents, provided they were willing and could afford it. It was customary for the parental contribution to be banked with the Head and, hopefully, disbursed on request. If John Kipling spent his school days in a state of penury, his lot was not unique. There were now five younger children in the Kipling family one of whom, his brother Joseph, was to join him at the Grove. The rest of the family comprised four girls, all younger than their brothers. John was not the only boy who lived out his school and college days on slender resources: his future brother-in-law, Edward Burne-Jones, admitted to his assistant, Thomas Rooke, that up to the age of eighteen years his pocket money only amounted to one penny a week.

If John Kipling was unhappy at school, and cocooned himself in an affectation of 'stoical apathy', he was far from being alone in his sufferings; rather he was one of a long line of distinguished men who passed through a similar Vale of Tears. William Cowper found Westminster, regarded as one of the most eminent of schools, a place of 'sheer torture and misery'. Edward Burne-Jones, a day-boy at the King Edward Free School, Birmingham, described himself, during his early days there, as 'the kind of little boy you

21

kick if you are a bigger boy' - and he was stabbed in the groin during prayers![20] Yet, despite his experiences at a great public school, Burne-Jones still sent his son, Philip, to Marlborough where he, in his turn, was unhappy. Even the ebullient Winston Churchill recalled his days at Harrow with a sense of revulsion, although he admitted that he may have been an exception to the general rule in the dislike which his recollections evoked.[21] Life in a public school a hundred years ago involved some harsh experiences, especially for an introspective and sensitive youth like John Kipling. Yet, despite the hardships he endured during his seven years there, and unlike Churchill at Harrow and William Morris at Marlborough, Kipling left the Grove grateful for the grounding he had received and, what was more important, with a desire to go on learning.

During the nineteenth century there were never more than a hundred and sixty boys at the Grove, including 'day-boys'. Out of so modest an intake, it is interesting to note how many of those became distinguished in a variety of fields.

Among her alumni there was numbered Sir William Atherton QC, Attorney-General and Legal Adviser to Her Majesty's Government. In law and politics there was Sir Henry Hartley Fowler, a friend of Alice Kipling's parents, who later became Lord Wolverhampton. During his time, as Secretary of State for India, he was accustomed to join the Queen at Balmoral where one of his duties (he was a handsome man) was to kiss the Royal cheek goodnight! To the political left was given Joseph Rayner Stephens, the Chartist leader.

Others who achieved distinction were Spencer Leigh Hughes, MP, more distinguished as 'leader writer' for the *Daily News* and the *Morning Leader*. To science, the Grove gave George Morley, FRCS, who discovered the qualities of strychnine and was a pioneer in the field of forensic medicine. One of John Kipling's contemporaries was William Fiddian Moulton, Head of Leys School, Cambridge and, in 1884, one of the revisers of the Old Testament. Like John Kipling, he became the father of a famous son for James Hope Moulton was a most distinguished Biblical scholar and the only Christian ever to be invited to lecture to the Bombay Parsee community on their religion, Zoroastrianism. By an odd coincidence it was the benevolence of the Parsees which provided the Bombay School of Art where John Kipling became an instructor.[22] Other notable scholars included Thomas Hodge Gross, Scholar of Balliol, President of the Oxford Union and Dean of Queen's College; J.M. Strachan, who became Bishop of Rangoon; and Theophilus B. Rowe, Fellow of St John's, Cambridge, who was Head of Tonbridge School from 1875 to 1890.

One of the more remarkable products of the Grove was George Scott Railton, another of Kipling's contemporaries. He became William Booth's lieutenant and devised the title 'Salvation Army'. He gave the Army its international links by leading its advance, first into the United States of America and, subsequently, to other parts of the world.[23]

The school produced men who, whilst contemporaries, found contrasting destinies! John Kipling grew up to reject the 'faith of his fathers' whilst George Scott Railton was to prove himself an outstanding leader in a Christian crusade.

Kipling left his school to become a designer, an artist, a journalist, a teacher of arts and crafts and a good servant of India and its peoples. Despite all the hardships, the tyrannies and the loneliness he suffered during his schooldays, he emerged a singularly humane and well-balanced young man - and 'the Pater' to his son, Rudyard Kipling.

References Chapter Two

1. KA 3/19
2. Pritchard p.5
3. Pritchard p.6
4. Pritchard p.13
5. Pritchard p.89
6. Pritchard p.107
7. *Letters of James Macdonald* p.106
8. *Age of Reform* - Woodward p.485
9. Pritchard p.128
10. *Pioneer* 26/9/1870
11. Pritchard p.115
12. Pritchard p.63
13. Pritchard p.64
14. *William Morris* - J Lindsey p.25
15. Pritchard p.83
16. Pritchard p.158
17. *Pilgrimage of Passion* p.9
18. *Something of Myself*
19. Pritchard p.167
20. *Edward Burne-Jones* - P.Fitzgerald p.18
21. *My Early Life* - W.S.Churchill
22. *The Treasure of the Magi and Early Zoroastrianism* - J.H.Moulton
23. *The General next to God* - R.Collier p.65

4.   Rudyard Lake, near Leek in Staffordshire *(where Alice and John shared a family picnic)*

Burslem - Apprenticeship

With John Kipling's school-days nearing an end, his parents must have begun to wonder what trade or profession their eldest child would be inclined to follow.

Whilst it would have been natural had they hoped that one day he might follow in his father's footsteps and join the ranks of the Wesleyan ministry, he was far too young for such a step. In 1851 the Wesleyans had opened the Westminster College for the training of teachers but, for economic reasons, attendance there was out of the question: their second boy Joseph was still at the Grove and there were four younger sisters at home, whose ages ranged between four and twelve years. It was essential that at the earliest possible date John should become a bread-winner or at least able to provide for his own physical needs.

The problem was unexpectedly resolved by a visit to the Great Exhibition held in Hyde Park between the first day of May and 11 October 1851. John travelled there by means of one of those cheap rail excursions, run by Mr Thomas Cook and others, which enabled millions of the working population of England to visit the Exhibition and see London for the first time.

The Great Exhibition was acclaimed by Queen Victoria as the Prince Consort's greatest achievement and she confided in her journal[1] that she felt proud of 'what her beloved Albert's great mind had conceived.' It would have been fairer and more accurate if she had written what her husband had 'achieved' rather than 'conceived' for the idea of an exhibition of such size and grandeur originated in the mind of Henry Cole, one of the outstanding public servants of the age.

The idea first took shape in Henry Cole's mind when he returned from the Quinquennial Exhibition held in Paris in 1849, determined to organise a different and more outstanding one in London.

His aim was to raise the standards of Industrial Art by persuading good painters and sculptors to produce designs for every-day articles in which beauty and utility were joined through good design. One of the chief differences between this and other exhibitions was that it would be international in scope.

Henry Cole was helped in the task of translating his dream into reality by the fact that, having begun his public life in the Public Records Office, he had become President of the Fine Arts Society and had already been awarded a medal for his design for a tea-service; thus it was the strength of his established reputation which enabled him to secure both the interest and patronage of the Prince Consort and, through him that of the Queen.

When Joseph Paxton's enormous creation, the Crystal Palace, as it came to be called, arose, the critics foretold that it would be a source of danger to the visitors on account of its construction of glass and iron: the first hail-stones which attacked it would result in destruction and inevitable casualties! Others professed concern over the great elm trees which Paxton had enclosed within his palace and prophesied that the 'five million sparrows' which would roost there would ruin both the exhibits and the clothing of the visitors with their droppings.

As it happened, the only problems which had to be faced arose from the success of the Exhibition and the inability of London's hotels, inns and boarding houses to cope with the demands made upon them. The chaos led to ordinary people seeking shelter in doorways or camping on the street, to which acts of vagrancy the police turned a blind eye. Even the gentry were forced, in many cases, to spend the night in their carriages (the horses having been unharnessed and taken away) with the result that powdered footmen were to be seen preparing breakfast on the pavements and Hay Hill and Berkeley Square were made fragrant with the smell of bacon and eggs!

John Kipling was more fortunate than most in this respect. His father had arranged for him to stay near Manchester Square with one of his ministerial colleagues, the Revd Alexander Strachan, whose son, John M. Strachan, had left Woodhouse Grove School the very year that Kipling entered. It was in this fashion that John approached what was to prove, in more ways than one, a water-shed in his life.

When William Morris was taken with his family to the Exhibition he refused to go in: one glance at the enormous creation made him declare it to be 'wonderfully ugly' and to remain outside. It was not so with John Kipling: he entered and found it not 'a length of cheerless monotony, iron and glass, glass and iron' (as his brother-in-law, Burne-Jones did) nor even, as the Queen described it, 'a fairy-like scene of enchantment', but a wonder-house, crammed with an absolute multiplicity of arts and crafts. When he left, his boyish mind was quite dazed by the overwhelming volume of what he had seen, from McCormick's Reaping Machine to strange shapes of lighthouses and models of bridges and galleries filled with jewelry, gorgeous satins, porcelain, carpets and glass-ware, in bewildering profusion. The all-important feature of this visit was that it determined the future course of his life for he came away with the conviction that he must become a craftsman and an artist.

As a child he had already shown a flair for handicrafts and had even made himself a pair of ice skates, with tapes instead of straps and rims made out of an old school slate, although in a letter to his grandson (also John) he admitted he did not think they could have been much use.[2] It is not surprising that he was drawn towards a career which would enable him to create beautiful and useful things.

The next problem confronting his father would be where to send his son in order that his ambitions might be realised - and how to afford it! That a solution to both these problems was found was owed at least in part to what the Methodists knew as 'the Brotherhood of the Ministry'.

During the years spent by the Kiplings in Howden, at least one of the Woodhouse Grove pupils had fulfilled the hopes of its founders and followed his father into the ranks of the Wesleyan ministry: his name was Edward Bourne Pinder. His appointment in 1843 was to Hornsea, in the same Methodist District as Howden, so that through meeting in the Synod twice a year he and Joseph Kipling were bound to have become acquainted. Edward's brother, Thomas (also a product of Woodhouse Grove) had, on leaving school, joined the family firm of Pinder, Bourne and Company, Earthenware Manufacturers of Burslem, Staffordshire. Through this chain of events, John was not only taken on in the role of apprentice with Pinder Bourne's but also enrolled as a student of the recently founded Stoke and Fenton Art School.

Such a solution to their problems must have come as quite a comfort to John's parents. After all, both at school and at home, he had led what in Staffordshire would be called 'a caded (sheltered) life' and his arrival in the Potteries must have constituted his introduction to the harsh realities of industrial life.

Again, the Pinder family was prominent in the life of Swan Bank Wesleyan Chapel, Burslem; there were several boys and girls in the family so that, as well as being able to enjoy the society of young people, John would be under the watchful eye of their parents.

A further advantage was the presence in Stoke-on-Trent of the new Art School and the possibilities of an extension of their son's education, especially in the field of arts and crafts. The Head, Silas Price, had, as one of his assistants, Albert Carrier, a Frenchman, later to be succeeded by his fellow-countryman, Hugues Protat. As classes took place in the afternoon and evening, it was possible to gain practical experience through work in the factory, and instruction in art and the technical aspects of the staple industry of the district later in the day. The place to which John Kipling came, and the kind of life to which he was introduced, have been classically described by Arnold Bennett, himself a native of the Potteries. In his *Anna of the Five Towns*, he reflects on the life of the district and of the chapel folk in the midst of which Kipling was to spend the next few years.

The valley in which the 'five towns' came to be strung together to form a city of a quarter of a million inhabitants, had once been 'one of the fairest spots in King Alfred's England'. By 1850 it had become defaced by industry. From the surrounding hills it looked like 'a smoke-girt amphitheatre' in which 'the grass still grew though it was not green' and where a farm, hedged about with furnaces, still harvested the sooty sheaves, whilst the smoke from ovens and furnaces stopped Agnes' gilly-flowers from growing.[3]

From Arnold Bennett's description of a revivalist meeting in Swan Bank Chapel it is easy to see how, in later years, John came to write the oft-quoted words: 'I have bowed my head in baize-lined pews of dissent... I have

27

marvelled at the ravings of Methodist ranters round weeping and snuffling victims at the penitent bench'.[4] The critical yet compassionate mind of the young man must have revolted against these examples of religious excess which Bennett described.[5]

With the hours he spent in the factory and attendance at the Art School it does not appear that John had much spare time on his hands. He must have been studiously inclined, for not only did he manage to win prizes in connection with his art studies, but he also accumulated a wealth of knowledge on a variety of subjects not strictly related to his profession.

Life in Burslem was not 'all work and no play': in later life John was able to write enthusiastically of the hours he spent skating on the frozen Staffordshire canals. In a letter to his grandson he said: 'Skating is, next to flying, the most delightful mode of motion possible, and long-distance skating better than figure skating.'[6]

In the summer there were picnics to local beauty spots, many of which lay within easy reach of Burslem; there were social gatherings in the homes of people like the Pinder's and the Benjamin Cork's, all well-to-do manufacturers where doubtless they gathered round the piano to sing Victorian ballads; to join in the singing of glees and, of course, in the singing of the hymns of Wesley and Watts. Certainly, when the time came for John to move to London, in pursuit of professional advancement, he missed the society of the Staffordshire people and the warm-hearted hospitality of which they were capable. He never lost touch with them and during the years of his retirement he was pleased to be invited back to lecture to his old Art School.

Having completed his Art School course with honours, Kipling moved to London in order to enlarge his practical experience. His first lodgings overlooked what was then the Millbank Penitentiary and is now the Tate Gallery. The penitentiary was supposed to be a model prison but to John it represented a 'geometrical night-mare'. When he looked back on those early days, he remembered the feeling of compassion aroused as, 'smoking a pipe in this eyrie, I saw at times working-parties of two or three figures clad in dingy brown, listless by doing nothing with rakes, barrows and besoms'.[7] Lonely during his school days, he was even more lonely in that vast city and, years afterwards, as he loaded his pipe with his favourite brand of tobacco, 'Lone Jack', he pondered as to whether the original 'Lone Jack' was 'any more alone than the rest of Johns, each perched on his own inaccessible island of loneliness'.[8]

John Kipling's early professional life has been well researched by James Craig.[9] His researches were centred around a letter dated 3 December 1864 addressed to the Chief Secretary to the Bombay Government. The writer was C.J. Erskine, a judge of the Bombay High Court who, during his furlough, had been asked to help 'in the recruitment of men to fill three newly-created posts for practising artist-craftsmen' in the Bombay School of Art, already in existence.[10]

The description given in that letter of John Kipling's qualifications suggests that, on arrival in London, he found employment with a well-known architectural sculptor, J. Birnie Philip. He assisted Philip in work on St Michael's, Cornhill; he also did some modelling for the Exeter College Chapel, Oxford and for the new church of All Souls, Halifax. All these projects were to G. Gilbert Scott's designs and, in James Craig's view, John must have worked as an 'art-workman' and carried out in stone ideas modelled by the directing architect and artist.[11] He was also associated with another prolific sculptor of the period, John Thomas.

C.J. Erskine's letter continued by saying that from 1860 to 1864 Kipling was 'in the service of the Department of Science and Art at South Kensington and most of the modelling for the terracotta decorations of the Museum had been executed by him.'[12] He was specially qualified for this task, not only on account of his practical knowledge of Gothic as well as Italian decoration, but also because of his acquaintance with the various processes of pottery.

Terracotta (baked earth) was a hard, unglazed pottery-fabric used for bricks, tiles and, increasingly, for architectural decorations, the latter on account of its ability to resist the soot and grime of an industrialised community. Its use for architectural decoration was still experimental in John Kipling's time and its production was largely in the hands of the firm of Minton with factories in Stoke and Burslem. It seems quite possible that, during his years in Burslem, John had become acquainted with Herbert Minton and thus was in a position to become the go-between for the designer and the manufacturer. This situation would account for his ability to retain his contacts with the museum even after his return to Burslem, following the death of his father.

Sir Henry Cole, whose Great Exhibition had first inspired in the young Kipling the ambition to become an artist and craftsman became, to a considerable degree, responsible for the building of the new Science Museum. Having confounded all his detractors and made a profit of nearly a quarter of a million from the Great Exhibition he had arranged the purchase of a piece of land in South Kensington and in 1860 secured a grant of £17,000 for the construction of the museum which, in 1899, came to be known as the 'Victoria and Albert'.

One of the designers was Geoffrey Sykes, formerly an assistant at the Sheffield Art School, and he was responsible for the revival of the use of terracotta in architectural decoration: it was in association with Sykes that Kipling worked on the new building. His contribution must have been appreciated because, in Sykes' celebrated terracotta plaque in the quadrangle of the museum may be seen, not only Henry Cole and other leading lights connected with the construction but, among the lesser lights, quite unmistakably, John Kipling, beard and all!

It was while John was working on the new museum that a young architect, Thomas Hardy, was at work in the old 'Brompton Boilers' (as the former Science Museum was called). His subject for a prize essay was 'The Application of Coloured Bricks and Terra Cotta to Modern Architecture'. It would

29

have been surprising if the two young men had not met. Not only did they share an interest in the use of terracotta for ornamentation but they both possessed literary leanings, and so had much in common as well as being contemporaries.[13] Hardy's employer, Sir Arthur Blomfield, was the son of the Bishop of London at a time when church restoration was in full swing and in which Kipling's associates, J. Birnie Philip and John Thomas, were also involved.

Whether the two young men became acquainted or not, is not clear but when John's son Rudyard came to London, and was a candidate for election to the Saville Club, he had the support, among others, of Thomas Hardy. Some years later when in search of 'a place in the country' he, in company, with Hardy, cycled around the Dorset countryside looking for a suitable house and even considered the purchase of one in Rodmell, Weymouth. Had he done so, might not Kipling have joined Hardy in extolling the beauties of Dorset rather than those of Sussex?

As was the case in Burslem, so now in London, John's time was not altogether devoted to the practise of his profession. He emerged from those years not only as an expert craftsman but with a considerable knowledge of a wide variety of other subjects; these included literature, art and even heraldry. He was blessed with the rare faculty of being able to recall almost anything he had heard or seen and his knowledge was not only extensive; it was accurate too.

John's daughter, Trix, often severely critical of her parents, claimed that her father 'knew something about everything and everything about some things'. At the same time, in the opinion of his brother-in-law, Frederic Macdonald, John made no show of his knowledge or oppressed one with it.[14]

It was shortly after John's arrival in London that his father, the Revd Joseph, died. He was only fifty five but his life of unremitting labours in 'the most toilsome of circuits' and exposure to bleak climatic conditions (especially those of the Pateley Bridge area), must have undermined his constitution. It was during the last years of his active ministry that he fainted in the vestry of his church and, as he was regaining consciousness, was amused to discover that instead of seeking to restore him, his church officials were composing his obituary. One said 'poor chap, he's gone to his reward'; 'Amen', said the other, 'The Lord's will be done!' Joseph survived this attack and shortly afterwards retired to Skipton along with his wife and four daughters. He continued to preach and his last sermon was given in December 1861. A few weeks later, in January 1862, Joseph also 'went to his reward'.

The death of his father at so early an age led directly to another critical phase in John Kipling's life. He returned to Burslem in order to give financial support to his widowed mother with several unmarried daughters on her hands. The eldest, Jane Frances, never married and there were, at the time of their father's death, three other girls whose ages ranged between thirteen and eighteen. A few years later they opened a little school in Skipton but in 1862 their position must have been somewhat parlous.

Once again the Pinders of Burslem came to the rescue and John found a post there as a modeller and designer - 'designing patterns and shapes for manufacturers and increasing his knowledge of plastic art'.[15]

In the same year, 1862, two ministerial appointments were made by the Wesleyan Conference. The first moved the Revd George Browne Macdonald and his family from Manchester to Wolverhampton: the second sent his son Frederic to his first appointment - at Swan Bank Wesleyan Chapel, Burslem. Many years later, as he looked back over his life, John's son Rudyard said that 'it seemed to him as though every card in his working life had been dealt to him in such a manner that he had but to play it as it came'.[16] Whether by this opening sentence he intended to imply a belief that 'there's a divinity that shapes our ends, rough-hew them how we will',[17] it is impossible to say but a study of the coming together of the lives of John Kipling and Alice Macdonald could easily suggest something more than the mere concatenation of circumstances. There was something almost uncanny in the manner in which their destinies came to be linked, although the cynic in John, rather than attributing it to the working of providence, would have been more likely to blame it on 'the long arm of coincidence'.

John Kipling was already at work in the Pinder Bourne factory when Frederic Macdonald and he first met. Only thirty five miles away lived four of Fred's five lovely sisters and the Pinders were glad to entertain them when they came to visit their brother. Soon after Frederic's arrival in Burslem, in the autumn of 1862, he was happy to introduce his sister Alice to his new friend 'who soon became her friend also'.[18] The traditions of the Macdonald family have described the first meeting of Alice with her future husband. It seems that she was being given 'a tour of the works' and, whilst waiting for a lift, the door shot open and a young man with golden beard and a receding hair-line emerged. He raised his hat, thus revealing his incipient baldness and was introduced.

Various people claimed responsibility for the famous picnic at Rudyard Lake which followed this meeting and which must have taken place in the early summer of 1863. Fred Macdonald only spoke of a day 'a number of us spent at Rudyard Lake, a favourite place of resort', after which John and Alice became engaged. Descendants of the Pinder family claimed it was their grandmother who gave the picnic: Fred's daughter, Florence, understood it was Fred himself who gave it to honour his sister who was on a visit at the time, but questioned the romantic details which attached themselves to accounts of that days proceedings. She admitted that her father received many kindnesses from the Pinder family, so the Pinder claim is probably nearest to the truth.[19]

So far as these 'romantic details' are concerned, the only reliable witnesses were, of course, the couple most intimately involved. John's account (which his children always suspected was part-fiction and to be taken with the proverbial pinch of salt) ran that, as he looked across the picnic, spread out on the grass, he observed a lovely creature, 'perversely engaged in consuming

31

a spring onion and knew that his fate was sealed'. Afterwards they strolled together and came across a gaunt grey horse in a field. John quoted Browning's *Childe Roland to the Dark Tower came*, 'Cast out past service from the Devil's stud'; Alice responded with the next line, 'He must have been wicked to deserve such woe!'

Later, during the same visit, they were reading poetry together (poetry moved John in the way that music moves other people) and he felt impelled to stoop down and kiss Alice who, with her 'track record' of three previous engagements, cannot have been a stranger to this manner of human communication; yet, she responded 'with absolute simplicity and gentleness'.

The conventions of the day demanded that John should seek her parents' permission before they could become officially engaged and, at the time of his arrival in Waterloo Road, Wolverhampton, the family were gathering for prayers. Just as John was announced, Mr Macdonald was about to read a passage from the first chapter of St John's gospel:'There was a man sent from God whose name was John'; the family claimed it was a good augury and so it proved to be through forty years of married life.

The year 1864 was well advanced without any definite date having been fixed for the wedding, most probably because John's wages were insufficient even to keep Alice 'in the manner of life to which she had been accustomed'. But help was not far away and it was only a matter of weeks before an envoy, C.J. Erskine, arrived from India in search of artist-craftsmen to teach at the School of Art, Bombay, which had been founded ten years before through the beneficence of a wealthy Parsee, Jamsetjee Jeejeebhoy. It was in this fashion that on 14 January 1865 John signed an agreement in the presence of Judge C.J. Erskine to work there. A bronze plaque in Bombay commemorates him as the School's 'first Principal' but this is not correct. He was a teacher of architectural sculpture and design and, three years later, he was driven to assert his independence and sole responsibility for the conduct of his own atelier, 'whatever Mr Terry's title of Acting Superintendent may mean!'

Under the terms of this agreement John was committed to the specialised study of the art of moulding and the use of terracotta pottery and ceramic manufactures in connection with building and ornamental sculpture. This further study was to be under the direction of Francis Wollaston Moody of the Department of Science and Art, South Kensington and during this period he was to be paid £3.17s.0d (£3.85p) a week. To estimate the present-day equivalent is not easy but it may be compared with the £160 a year paid to Alice's father and the £120 received by John's. The use of a house, rent and rates were free and were added to the basic stipends in both cases and both ministers had contrived to bring up large families, without ever finding themselves in debt. Thus the figure of nearly £200 a year must have seemed to Alice and John an adequate sum on which to get married.

The prospect of life in India did not commend itself either to the Kipling family or the Macdonalds. It was only a few years since the horrors of the

Indian Mutiny had filled the newspapers; India was the other side of the world and notorious for its climate and diseases. Alice's brother, Harry, had passed for the Indian Civil Service but had not taken up his appointment owing to the reluctance of his fiancée, Peggy Talboys, to go there. Yet the opportunity was too good to miss; Alice at twenty eight was, according to Victorian ideas, getting old for marriage. Thus, on 14 January 1865, John signed the contract, using for the first time the name by which he came to be known, John Lockwood Kipling, though to his family and friends he was always known as John.

The contract into which he entered was for a period of three years during which he was to be paid at the rate of four hundred rupees a month, the equivalent of £400 a year. In addition he was to receive an additional ten rupees for each pupil or apprentice he taught, the total not to be in excess of one hundred and twenty rupees a month. He accepted these terms, although he only expected to be able to provide his family with a bare subsistence.

Two months later, on a cold day in March, Alice's mother Mrs Macdonald called at Reynold's Cafe, High Green, Wolverhampton and ordered the despatch of two fowls and a veal cake to Mrs E.B. Jones, Kensington Square, London. This was to be her husband's contribution to his daughter's wedding breakfast for, owing to his illness, neither he nor his wife was able to attend. He sent a message to his daughter, Georgiana Burne-Jones, asking her to accept the viands as 'a little token of his love' and so, on a snowy fourth day of March, the marriage of Alice and John was celebrated in the old St Mary Abbott Church, Kensington. Frederic Macdonald gave his sister away and among the guests were Alice's two unmarried sisters, Agnes and Louie, who had to wait for 1866 before they were able to share a double-wedding in St Peter's Collegiate Church, Wolverhampton. Mrs Joseph Kipling came from Skipton to see her son married and was accompanied by two of her daughters, Jane and Ruth. The 'best man' was Henry Longden, one of John's friends from the South Kensington, whilst the artistic and literary life of London was represented by Dante Gabriel Rossetti, Algernon Swinburne, Ford Madox Brown and, of course, Edward Burne-Jones from whose home the bride was married.

On his way to his lodging in Pelham Street, after the wedding breakfast, John managed to lose his key and to leave his money behind but, with the aid of a hansom cab, the newly married pair were safely delivered at the railway station and on their way to honeymoon in Yorkshire.

After honeymooning for three weeks in Skipton, John and Alice returned to Wolverhampton on the first day of April and ten days later were off to Southampton to board the s.s. *Ripon*, a paddle- steamer, bound for Alexandria. The Suez Canal still belonged to the future and they had been directed to take the overland route to India via Alexandria, Zagazig and Suez; then another ship to Bombay.

It had been the intention of Rossetti to give a dinner in honour of his friends but, unfortunately, he had the decorators in at 16 Cheyne Walk and eventually the dinner became a luncheon because the host was 'short on tin'. By that time John and Alice were well advanced on their four weeks' journey to Bombay.

References Chapter Three

1. *Journal* 22.2.1850
2. KA 1/5
3. *Anna of the Five Towns* - Arnold Bennett p.24, 25
4. *Inezilla* - J.L. Kipling p.75
5. *Anna of the Five Towns* p.60
6. KA 1/5
7. *Pioneer* August 1870
8. KA 1/10
9. KJ December 1974, March 1975
10. KJ March 1975
11. KJ December 1974
12. KJ March 1975
13. *The Young Thomas Hardy* - R. Gittings p.100
14. *As a Tale that is Told* - F.W. Macdonald p.335
15. *As a Tale that is Told* - F.W. Macdonald p.114
16. *Something of Myself* p.1
17. *Hamlet* 1V, ii
18. *As a Tale that is Told* - F.W. Macdonald p.115
19. Letter to Margaret Mackail - 4.11.1939

Courtship and Marriage

As Alice Kipling (née Macdonald) stood on the deck of the paddle-steamer s.s. *Ripon* and watched the English coastline recede over the horizon, she must have come close to understanding the feelings of the characters portrayed by her friend, Ford Madox Brown, in his picture *The Last of England*.

Not only was she finally separated from the large and affectionate family in which she had grown up; she was leaving behind an invalid father she might never see again. On the other hand, being possessed of a sanguine nature and an adventurous disposition, there can be no doubt that she looked forward with eager anticipation to her life in India.

Her mother was one of the founder members of the Methodist 'Women's Auxiliary' (as it was then known), a missionary committee whose members were accustomed to speak of distant lands as though they were merely adjacent counties. Alice had dutifully attended missionary meetings and had often sung Bishop Heber's hymn about 'India's coral strand'; she had heard from missionaries on furlough of India's beauty, horrors, perils and the colourful variety of its teeming population. It is true that, so far as Alice was concerned, expectation was to exceed realisation and she never came to love India in the same way as did her husband. On that April day in 1865, as the s.s. *Ripon* headed down Channel, bound for Alexandria, there is no doubt that she looked forward eagerly to her first encounter with 'the Mysterious Orient'.

Alice's family believed they were descended from the Macdonalds of Skye, several contingents of whom had fled to Ireland after the catastrophe which befell them at Culloden Moor in 1746. It was the Clan Macdonald which had first welcomed the Young Pretender, Prince Charles Edward, on his return from exile; it was they who had enabled him to escape following the defeat of his ill-fated rebellion. Some of the clan emigrated to North America, some to Northern Ireland and it was there, at Ballynamallard, that Alice's grandfather, James Macdonald, was born in 1761.

The political tides which so shaped Scottish history during the first half of the eighteenth century were matched by those of the Evangelical Revival which swept England and Wales during the same years. The first upheaval took the Macdonalds from their highland crofts and glens to Ireland; the second prised John Wesley out of his comfortable life as a Fellow of Lincoln College, Oxford, to become a travelling evangelist and, in pursuit of his mission, to arrive in Ireland too. It was there in 1784 that Wesley called young James Macdonald to join his band of Methodist Preachers.

After some years of service in the land of his birth, James was summoned to cross the Irish Channel and minister in Chester. Like an obedient son, he

5. Alice Macdonald *(courtesy of The Kipling Society)*

came bringing with him his wife, Anne Browne, whom he had met whilst ministering in Newry. They subsequently moved to London and James was appointed Assistant Editor of the *Methodist Magazine*: it was there that, having borne her husband four children, Anne died and was laid to rest in the little graveyard at Wesley's Chapel, City Road.

Anne's youngest child, George Browne Macdonald, grew up to become a strikingly handsome youth, gregarious yet of a studious nature. He was one of the first pupils at the newly opened Wesleyan Academy for the sons of the ministry at Apperley Bridge, known as Woodhouse Grove[1] and during his earlier years had the Revd Patrick Brontë as his examiner. So well did he profit by his studies that he was the first pupil to be invited to spend an extra year at the school, provided he undertook teaching duties. Then followed a few years of secular employment before George joined his father as a Methodist minister in the Devonport Circuit.

Like his father, George Macdonald suffered the sorrows of bereavement, through the death of his first wife Mary A'Court, but a few years later was appointed to Manchester where he met and married Hannah Jones, the daughter of a well-to-do wholesale-grocer of Cannon Street. They had eleven children of whom seven survived to maturity: Alice was the eldest of five surviving sisters.

Her mother, Hannah Macdonald, was a woman of above average education whose family hailed from the Vale of Clwyd. This infusion of Welsh blood made Alice 'pure Celt and all fire'; possibly it was their Welsh blood (sometimes overlooked) which accounts for that 'decided touch of the elegiac' which John was to note in all the Macdonald sisters.[2]

The family in which Alice grew up was quite unlike the pictures of Victorian clerical families, so beloved of novelist and playwright. Far from being gloomily pious and morally restrictive, their home echoed and re-echoed to the sound of laughter and music. Alice had her faults but dullness was not one of them; nor was the tribute of being, in *Plain Tales from the Hills*, 'the wittiest woman in India', undeserved.

Her father George Macdonald was a man of wide culture and great tolerance. He used to say that 'he was never so much a Methodist as to forget he was first a Christian and, provided his children grew up to be good Christians, he cared not that they were Methodists or not.' This was just as well because, of his seven children, only Frederic remained loyal to the church of his fathers. He was to follow his father into the ranks of the ministry but was always something of a rebel. His father had been persuaded to side with the 'new-fangled' arguments in favour of total abstinence from the consumption of alcoholic beverages and had written a pamphlet on the subject;[3] yet, whilst advocating the new 'teetotalism', he warned his readers against the temptation to self-righteousness. Fred, on the other hand, enjoyed his glass of port and big cigar!

George Macdonald was also a man of considerable physical courage: during his years in Devonport he had saved a man from drowning in Plymouth

Sound and in London had gone to the aid of a policeman who was being assailed by a gang of roughs.

The wide tolerance which was one of his characteristics appeared in the fact that when three of his daughters chose to marry artists - Edward Burne-Jones, John Kipling and Edward Poynter (it was as an artist that John Kipling described himself on his marriage certificate) - their father raised no objection even though artists were generally regarded as leading 'bohemian' lives which meant, at best, unconventional ones.

As Frederic Macdonald looked back on his early days, when all the family were at home, his recollections were of genial relationships bewee parents and children which were always free and happy.[4] Although their father was respected, he was approachable and kind: he possessed a keen sense of humour and was 'a prince of story-tellers'. From his own father George had inherited an aversion to what was called 'evil-speaking' (meaning calumny) and when the family conversation tended in that direction, he would steer it away with an irrelevant enquiry regarding the price of potatoes.

Alice, the eldest of the Macdonald sisters, was of medium height, slenderly built with auburn hair, black eyelashes and blue-grey eyes which, according to her brother Fred, altered their colour with her changing emotions. She had a lovely soprano voice, wrote both poetry and music and succeeded in everything she undertook, whether it was in the realm of art, of needle-work, letter-writing or cookery. Passionately fond of music, she excelled both as a pianist and a singer.

Like her father, Alice was blest with a sanguine disposition and was never inclined to mourn over lost Edens. It was her usual cheerfulness which enabled her to cope with the rigours of the Indian climate and the irritations of Indian servants and, although she never really liked India, she remained there for nearly thirty years.

Both John and Alice possessed 'the faults of their virtues'. Her strength of character made her, at times, insensitive to the needs and feelings of others. Again, although she retained her girlish figure and youthful appearance well into middle-age, she was foolishly sensitive about her true age. (She was three months senior to her husband).

Her ready wit could sometimes take on a sharp and rather cruel edge: this appeared in some 'gossipy' letters she wrote home to her friend Editha Plowden. For instance, she could write that 'the brides of whom last year we were so proud are now rather a source of humiliation... Mrs Turton Smith is very much 'en evidence', nearly as big as her mother... she has a furtive look and almost guilty air, as if she had committed some crime and expected to be found out at any moment.' Again, 'Mrs Rivaz looks old enough to be her husband's mother!' Of Mrs Young, Alice wrote: 'you will be shocked to hear that she is going to perpetuate her kind.'

When Rudyard's name was linked with a Miss Parry-Lambert, Alice wrote that they used to think Mrs Black's daughter very plain until Mrs Parry-Lambert's daughter came out and, 'by her transcending ugliness, made Miss

Black seem almost beautiful. Mrs L. is greatly distressed about her daughter's appearance and no wonder!'[5]

John, although the kindest and gentlest of men, could at times match his wife's rather 'waspish' comments with some of his own. For example, when the Lieutenant-Governor's daughter became engaged, he wrote to Miss Plowden: 'Miss Egerton is to marry Mr Mackworth-Young, an undreamed of catch, for never, surely, went matrimonial hook into the depths so slenderly baited.'[6]

Alice seems to have been well-aware of the danger of allowing banter to degenerate into spitefulness and was very conscious of this fault in others. 'Spite', she wrote 'flourishes here like a kind of prickly pear, lining the lane of life,' and went on to confess that 'not possessing a light fantastic toe' of her own, she naturally 'jeered furiously at those of others!'[7]

Both John and Alice obviously enjoyed 'a spot of gossip' and John justified it as 'an absolute necessity.'

'Things interest us here only through persons,' he wrote; 'there is little else to furnish us with the gentle mental exercises of which we are capable... Thus the quarrel between Robinson and Green, which rages in official foolscap; the flirtation of Mrs Brown and Mr Jones, is my opera; the careful study of ladies' bonnets and dress in church has all the interest of the Royal Academy... these things, and many more, are provided by a bountiful Providence for the entertainment of mankind.'[8]

During one of John's absences on business, Alice undertook his journalistic task and one of her more acerbic comments was that 'in view of the difficulty of loving one's neighbour as one's self, some of us sought to compensate by loving our neighbour's wife better than our own!'[9]

Whether it was her intention to include her husband in this general statement is not clear but there are plenty of suggestions that she might well have been justified in so doing.

All his life John had shown himself an incorrigible flirt; even when he had achieved old age he deplored his tendency 'to think of old sweethearts' and confessed that he could not help it. In a letter to his friend Editha Plowden he wrote: 'In the reconstructed world of G.B. Shaw, J.W. Mackail and H.G. Wells there will be quite a new code of sexual manners and I would I were there to see it!'[10]

Before her engagement to John Kipling, Alice had three broken betrothals, two to William Allingham and one to William Fulford. According to Trollope, a broken engagement meant the loss of 'that precious delicacy which is the greatest treasure of womanhood'.[11] Her sister Edith complained that Alice never went away on a visit without coming back 'engaged to some cad of the desert'. Her father feared she was in danger of becoming known as a flirt.

Even when Alice reached middle-age and had a grown-up son and daughter, she enjoyed coquetting with the young men who came to Simla on duty or on leave and on one occasion, when the Viceroy, Lord Dufferin, asked her daughter Trix why she was not dancing, Trix replied 'because I'm only seventeen' adding that when she 'achieved forty', she 'would have some partners'; no doubt a shaft aimed at her mother who retained her girlish figure and escaped greying hair, right up to her middle years. It has been suggested that Rudyard's poem *My Rival*:

> The incense that is mine by right
> They burn before her shrine;
> And that's because I'm seventeen
> And she is forty-nine!

was prompted by his sister's resentment of her mother's popularity with the young men 'elegant in scarlet and gold'.[12]

Whatever reputation, deserved or undeserved, was earned by either John or Alice Kipling (or both of them), the fact remains that they remained devoted to each other for the whole of their life together. After ten years of marriage, Alice told Miss Plowden that they found separation harder to bear with each passing year and, after John recovered from a near-fatal attack of typhoid, which he only survived through the devotion of his wife, he wrote her 'a most moving out-pouring of love and gratitude'.

It is possible that the Kiplings were so sure of each other's affection that they could find amusement in occasional light-hearted flirtations, conducted without jealousy and without hurt to either partner.

Although Rudyard was the product of a mixing of Yorkshire blood with Celtic, he liked to regard himself as a Yorkshire tyke[13] and not a Celt; yet, despite his professed regard for Yorkshire, his portrayal of Yorkshire characters was never very flattering. One of his famous 'Soldiers Three', John Learoyd, he described as 'six and a half feet of slow moving, heavy footed Yorkshireman, born in the Wolds, bred in the Dales, educated among the carriers' carts at the back of York Station... accustomed to fight blindly at the bidding of a superior mind.'[14]

Even less flattering is Rudyard's portrait of Silas Riley: 'a long gawky, raw-boned Yorkshireman, full of the savage self-conceit that blossoms only in the best county in England',[15] whilst Nafferton shows all the characteristics of "a Dalesman from beyond Skipton who will forgive an injury when the Strid lets a man live" '.[16]

The question in search of an answer is surely: what was it that made Rudyard favour his paternal origins rather than those of his mother? Could it be that he found Alice less sympathetic than John and more dominating; harder, yet possessing that mystical side of the Celt which he feared to recognise in himself? 'If success comes,' he wrote to E.K. Robinson, who had succeeded Stephen Wheeler as editor of the *Civil and Military Gazette*, 'my father's delight will be greater than mine; if the money comes my mother will be more pleased than I!',[17] thereby suggesting that his mother was hard-headed and perhaps more hard-hearted than his father, who stands in complete contrast to most of Rudyard's delineations of Yorkshire character.

It is difficult to identify the mother who, in Rudyard's early days, refused to allow her maternal feelings to interfere with her literary judgement with the lush sentimentality of a poem like *'Mother O' Mine'* or, later, the short story entitled *The Brushwood Boy*.

So far as the former is concerned it should be remembered that, at the time of its writing, Rudyard was hovering on the brink of a nervous breakdown which finally sent him off to seek the popular cure of a sea-voyage.

This mental and physical breakdown had a variety of causes. Once he had found bachelor lodgings in Villiers Street he discovered (as had his father thirty years earlier) that London can seem like the loneliest place on earth: he believed himself the most heart-sick and thoroughly wretched man in the Metropolis. He missed the sunshine, the colour and the varied life of the Punjab where he had been a person in his own right and not a mere nonentity in the teeming life of a great city. Then he had met Florence Garrard, the object of his teenage worship and found that, although he was still gripped by his passion for her, she continued cold and unresponsive. In order to escape from the pangs of unrequited love, he had plunged himself into a veritable orgy of work: *Barrack Room Ballads,*, *The Light that Failed* and *Life's Handicap* were all the fruit of those shadowed days. *Mother O' Mine* was the dedicatory poem included with *The Light that Failed* when it was published in 1891 and just as a mortally-wounded soldier will cry out for his mother, so the stricken soul of young Kipling sought comfort in the thought of his own mother. Lines like 'If I were drowned in the deepest sea' suggest being lost in a sea of troubles; 'the sense of being damned in body and soul' is typical of the hallucinations which plague those who suffer acute depression, whilst 'If I were hanged on the highest Hill' suggests the need to expiate some feeling of guilt.

It is generally accepted that Mrs Lucy Hauksbee, Rudyard's famous character from the Simla scene, was modelled on Mrs Burton, a lady who played opposite Rudyard in Sardou's play *A Scrap of Paper*. But she could be a combination of both Mrs Burton and Alice Kipling. She is described as 'a glamorous mother-figure': she lives on familiar terms with the Viceroy (as did Alice) whilst her mission in life is to advance the prospects of those young men of whom she approved and to guard them from predatory females; just as Alice guarded her son!

Alice Kipling was in sympathy with John's rebellion against 'the faith of his fathers'. According to the family traditions, there had been an occasion when she took a family heir-loom and threw it on the fire with the words: 'There goes the hair of the dog that bit us!' The heir-loom was a reputed lock of John Wesley's hair! When the Lockwood Kiplings arrived in Bombay, it is plain that they associated themselves with the Cathedral, possibly because they recognised the social disadvantages of being Methodist. In John's words, 'The English lose caste when they become dissenters.' Thus, whilst they observed the outward forms of religion, they were those of the Church of England according to whose rites their first-born child was baptised 'Joseph Rudyard'.

41

The Pater

Whilst her husband became a complete and confirmed sceptic, it was not quite the case with Alice. During a visit to Tisbury by her brother, Frederic, she handed him, without comment, a paper on which were some lines she had written early in the morning: they were entitled *At the Dawn* and ran:

As from my window at first glimpse of dawn
I watch the rising mist that heralds day;
And see by God's strong hand the curtain drawn
That through the night has hid the world away;
So I, through windows of the soul, shall see
One day, Death's fingers, with resistless might,
Draw back the curtained gloom that shadows life.
And on the darkness of Time's deepest night,
Let in the perfect day - Eternity -[18]

References Chapter Four

1. Pritchard p.78
2. KA 1/10
3. *An Apology for the Dis-use of Alcoholic Beverages* - G.B. Macdonald
4. *As a Tale that is Told* - Fred Macdonald p.9
5. KA 1/11
6. KA 1/11
7. KA 1/11
8. *Pioneer Mail* 17.2.1876
9. *Pioneer Mail* 7.11.1870
10. *Pioneer Mail* 9.11.1909
11. *Can You Forgive Her* - A. Trollope
12. *My Rival* - Rudyard Kipling
13. Holograph in possession of Author
14. *Incarnation of Krishna Mulvaney* - Rudyard Kipling
15. *Plain Tales from the Hills - A Bank Fraud* - Rudyard Kipling
16. *Plain Tales from the Hills - Pig* - Rudyard Kipling
17. KA 17/25
18. *As a Tale that is Told* - F. Macdonald p.337

Bombay - A Blazing Beauty of a Place

Mr and Mrs Lockwood Kipling's first introduction to India was probably by way of their noses. Before coming within sight of land they would be met by a spicy smell, compounded of jasmine, frangipani, cow-dung smoke and that indispensible adjunct to Indian cuisine, turmeric. It was the same smell that greeted Rudyard when he returned to the sub-continent in December 1891 to spend Christmas with his parents. He wrote: 'A smell came up out over the sea - a smell of damp earth, coconut oil, ginger, onions and mankind'.[1]

Once the last lap of their voyage had been reached they found themselves sailing under blue skies up a noble water-way, studded with islands, lined with palm-fringed coasts. John's first impressions were such that his cautious Yorkshire soul was moved to describe Bombay as 'a blazing beauty of a place' and 'the most beautiful place in the world'!

But disenchantment was not far off and, having landed, the Kiplings found that their bungalow was not yet ready for occupation so that they began their life in India as 'dwellers in tents' on the beach. Eventually they were housed on a narrow neck of land with the sea to the West and the splendid harbour, crowded with the masts of shipping, to the East. The dazzling blue of sea and sky, the Arab dhows skimming the waters, the gaily dressed Parsees, the winds in the palm trees and banana trees, all combined to transport them into a new and exotic environment of scent, sound and colour; it must have seemed another world compared with the factories of Wolverhampton, the 'pea-soupers' of London and the kilns of Burslem.

The whole journey from Southampton had taken four weeks and to cover their expenses John had been given a grant of £200. About £100 of this went on the fares and the rest in the purchase of tropical outfits which, in the case of Alice, included cotton umbrellas and 'a desert hat of the foulest appearance.'

Parting with their families cannot have been without pain. India was largely a far-off and unknown land, the abode of tigers, snakes, monkeys and sepoys. Its dark-skinned people, were, in the 'popular' mind, capable of indescribable atrocities; it was cursed with all manner of foul diseases from which the wife of their friend Heeley and some of their parents' missionary colleagues, had died, and yet, although days were to come when she regretted it, Alice faced the unknown with a cheer: for her it was a great adventure, an exciting new way of life. To her weeping sisters she appeared insensible and unfeeling; in herself she thrilled with a pleasing sense of anticipation; by the time they landed she must have suspected she was pregnant.

The city of Bombay was already rivalling Calcutta, not only as a port (it was yet four years to the opening of de Lessep's Suez Canal which was to make Bombay the Gateway to India), but also as a great centre of industry and commerce.

Originally a group of seven off-shore, malaria-ridden islands, Bombay had come to Britain as part of the dowry of Catherine of Braganza on her marriage with Charles II. In the opinion of Samuel Pepys it was 'a poor little island' but with the passage of the years, the English appropriated the rest of the group and then rented them to the East India Company for a consideration of ten pounds in gold per year.

The real creator of British influence in India, and one whose work was to exercise a profound influence on John Kipling's life, was Gerald Aungier, Governor of Bombay 1669-77. Chivalrous and intrepid, he was also a man of great piety and possessed of considerable qualities of leadership. He saw Bombay as 'a city which, with God's assistance, is intended to be built'.[2]

Aungier came to Bombay from the original Company settlement up North at Surat when, under pressure from the marauding Mahrattis, trading became difficult. He showed himself a man of surprisingly liberal outlook and welcomed to the city men of all races, regardless of colour or creed. Thus, to the emerging city came Arab and Banian merchants, Jains and Gujeratis and, most vital of all, so far as the Kiplings were concerned, the Parsees; but for whose presence in Bombay they might never have come to India.

Like so many of the immigrants down the centuries who have fled to England, the Parsees came to Bombay as refugees from religious persecution. They had been driven from Persia, their native land, under pressure from Mahomet's militant followers. They first settled in Kujerat but were again driven to seek a refuge further South; thus in the seventeenth century they settled in Bombay and became involved in the commercial and industrial growth of that city.

The Parsees were followers of an Iranian reformer known as Zarathustra (or Zoroaster) who, 400 years before Christ, had tried to replace the primitive polytheism of Persia with a theological dualism which saw the earth as the battle-field between the opposing forces of Good and Evil; of Light and Darkness. The moral and ethical principles of their religion demanded the practice of an active benevolence. It was in pursuit of this principle that they founded hospitals, schools and colleges, one of their endowments being the Jeejeebhoy School of Art to which John Kipling came as a teacher of architectural sculpture, the art of moulding and the use of terracotta in connection with building.

Once settled in their new home the Kiplings began to discover some of the disadvantages of life in 'the mysterious East'. Their baggage, which had been consigned to the long sea-route, failed to materialise and they were compelled to buy a six-piece dinner service which cost John a week's wages. At the same time they discovered that the 'caste system' meant that they must employ what seemed to them to be a small army of servants. They had been told that labour was cheap in India and, meagre as the wages of English domestic servants were, Indian wages were lower. They learned that it took two or three natives to do the work of one good English servant and the service Alice got from her staff was a source of dissatisfaction: they showed themselves 'capable of curious attacks of fatuity'; 'the Eternal Now had no meaning for them'; at times they could be 'terrible blunderers and the dhobi wallah proved himself an expert in the art of dismembering fine linen and laces'.

One of the surprising features of those early days in Bombay was not that they found things to complain about but that their complaints were surprisingly few. There was no complaint about the swarming insect life or the abundance of vermin; no mention was made of the crude sanitary arrangements which must have horrified health-conscious Alice.

One aspect of their new life, with which the Kiplings failed to come to terms, was the climate. They were fortunate in that they arrived in Bombay before the onset of the Monsoon which, between June and September, was capable of releasing 250 inches of rain. The preceding weeks of high humidity must have proved very trying for them after the typical English Spring, with its flurries of snow, they had left behind. When the rains really came, John was moved to observe that 'in *Twelfth Night* it was only the Fool who found fun in the fact that the rain it raineth everyday!' Alice expressed her feelings in verse:

> Dull in the morning, duller still at noon,
> Dullest of all as dreary night draws round,
> I go from mildewed couch to mouldy bed
> And in the morning shall not feel surprise
> If from the reeking pillow, neath my head,
> I find a crop of mushrooms when I rise.

In the month of June, five years later, John (now Bombay Correspondent to the *Pioneer* in India) reported that 'the windows of heaven had opened to such an extent that my ancient belief in the Deluge was irresistibly confirmed'.[3] The climate 'brought rheumatism to the eyes and ague in all his limbs.' He complained, 'the steamy darkness increases day by day until one grows desperate and no more pretends to hide the fact that he is the moistest and most miserable of mortals.' Should any reader be disposed to contradict his report, he invited them to visit Bombay and listen to the big yellow frogs, baying like blood-hounds which led him to sympathise with the ancient Egyptians 'who had frogs in their bed-chambers and in their kneading troughs'[4].

Alice was disgusted to find toadstools growing in her bonnet and a cockroach nesting in her newest hat.

After the rains came the sun, 'that pitiless destroyer of youth and beauty', and John concluded that Bombay only had two seasons, the wet and the hot. He also called the sun 'that cruel terminator of delights in this country'. One day he discovered a little stream which reminded him of the becks of his native county. As he watched it pursue its merry way down from the hills, his thoughts turned to trout, a fishing rod, a fly-book and a pipe - mere illusions, 'to be dispelled by the rapidly rising sun'. Alice reckoned there were days when the sun just stood still, 'like Joshua's moon at Ajailon'.[5]

Following their arrival in India, one of the lessons the Kiplings had to learn, was the importance of protocol. Order of precedence was a constant subject of debate among the Anglo-Indians (as the British were then known). They lived under the yoke of the Civil List.

First in order of precedence came the senior members of the Indian Civil Service, the most highly paid civil servants in the world at the time. After them came the senior ranks of the Army; then the judges and government solicitors. The British merchant princes occupied a lowly place in 'the pecking order' and were often referred to contemptuously as 'box-wallahs', a name given by the natives to travelling salesmen. Not surprisingly the teacher of terracotta manufactures came even further down the order and discovered, when invited out, that he and his wife were expected to go in last to dinner. Their Lahore friend, Editha Plowden, somewhat naively thought they were not even aware of the situation and that if they were, they did not care. This is improbable, especially where Alice was concerned and it is likely that there were times when the situation rankled.

The striking feature of the whole situation was that, in spite of being socially disadvantaged, much later they eventually won an entrée into the very highest social circles, including the homes of the Commander-in-Chief and even the Viceroy.

Within a few months of coming to Bombay they found themselves being caught up in the social whirl. John wrote to tell Alice's sister, Edith Macdonald, that they had been to dinner with one of the Bombay clergy, a man called Fletcher, and there had met Lady Frere, the wife of the Governor, Sir Henry Bartle Frere. Not only had they been introduced to Lady Frere but also 'to various swells'. After dinner Alice had 'sung in the choruses and in the duets' just like a bird.[6]

It is at once apparent that life in the 'outposts of Empire' depended very much for its entertainment on the 'do-it-yourself' principle. Such an accomplished performer as Alice was soon in demand. One of Rudyard's childhood memories was of his mother 'singing wonderful songs at a black piano and going out to Big Dinners'.[7] The so-called 'Big Dinners' became so numerous that, on at least one occasion, Alice reported that, as she had not attended the St Andrew's Day dinner, she was not in a position to say 'in what respects it differed from the other three hundred and sixty four dinners which were held throughout the year.'

John had the responsibility of reporting for the *Pioneer* one of the most important social functions of the year, the annual ball of the Byculla Club. As the club had been enlarged and redecorated it was exceptionally bright that year and he regretted 'that age with its stealing steps had him tightly in its clutch' (he was 34). This put a brake on his participation but it did not prevent him and the rest of 'the old fogies from enjoying, for a brief space, the gorgeous coup d'oeil presented on that occasion.' What surprised him was that the notorious Byculla mosquitoes, which the previous year had hovered in clouds around the ladies' shoulders, had foreborn to bite. Had he been a mosquito, he decided, and confined to a meagre diet of broadcloth, bald heads and masculine knuckles for the rest of the year, he would have made the most of the opportunities presented on the festival night of the Ball.[8]

As well as the succession of dinners and balls, there was the Philharmonic Society. Its musical tastes were not always of the highest quality and it tended to concentrate on the bravura and sentimental ballads so beloved of the Victorians. This aberration did not coincide with the Kipling musical preferences but 'music was not the only interest which brought the members of the Philharmonic Society together and bound them in harmonious performance'; 'good wines and good dinners were part of every performance.'

The Philharmonic Society was not without its problems, one of which was the lack of a suitable building in which to meet and perform. John dubbed the Grant Theatre as being 'akin to a detestable dog-house' and when the Batavian and Italian Opera Company proposed to visit Bombay he warned them to stay away. 'We lack a suitable building for operatic performances,' he wrote and added that 'such entertainments do not thrive out here.' Whilst so doing he put in a plea for the building of a new theatre without which the European community would never take to play-going.

Besides lack of suitable accommodation, the Philharmonic Society was constantly faced with the problems peculiar to a transient society. John described the Anglo-Indian community as being 'like sands in the desert, ever changing'. He wrote: 'the doctor orders your best tenor to England on pain of his becoming a croaker if he remains; your bass mournfully leaves you to wake the echoes of a remote jungle solitude: your lovely soprano has to lead her infant chorus back to school via the P and O'.[9] Regarding the fate of the mature contralto, John refrained from comment!

As might be expected in a British community the round of social activities was never complete without those of an out-door and sporting nature. John reported invariably as a somewhat cynical observer rather than an active participant, or even an interested spectator. Sporting activities were never a strong card in the hand of a Kipling which may in part account for the scathing reference by Rudyard to 'the flannelled fools at the wicket, the muddied oafs at the goals'. Hence, John's somewhat amused and tolerant approach to such events! It is doubtful if the Kiplings joined the Bombay Sailing Club: in their early days an acquaintance had taken them in his boat down the harbour to inspect and sketch an eighteenth century pirates' lair. Unfortunately, when they tried to return, the winds proved contrary and it was not until the early hours of the morning that they made port. Alice declared that from then on 'she would never set foot on anything that floats.' Despite this prejudice, it fell to John's lot to report on the Regatta. The artist in him responded to the sight of half a dozen boats 'spreading their white

47

wings in swift flight over the waves' but he soon found the occasion somewhat tedious. 'To enjoy a regatta,' he observed, 'calls for a nautical, or "yachtical", taste and, without a dash of salt water in the veins, it was impossible to watch the competitors for three hours in breathless suspense'. Characteristically he found compensation in 'a balcony full of lovely and gracious ladies in fair colours and textures' and managed to enjoy the scene, 'flashing with light and colour'.[10]

If the Regatta failed to kindle John's enthusiasm, so did the Races. Regretfully he wrote 'some are born horsey but few, by taking thought, achieve horsiness'. Here again the artist in him found consolation 'in the springy horses, the bright shirts of the jockeys and the presence of lovely ladies'.

The game of polo had not, in the seventies of the last century, achieved the social prestige it enjoys today. John even dared to refer to it somewhat irreverently as 'hockey on horse-back'. He admired the clever ponies as they wheeled, twisted and turned and, as a craftsman, he was interested in what he called 'the bamboo clubs' which the riders wielded with 'their cross pieces set on diagonally'.[11] Yet on the whole he showed scant interest in equine sports which cannot have added to his popularity in a society where the horse was venerated almost as an object of worship. Nor did John Kipling ever find himself in the grip of the golfing fever. 'I can see the point of many diversions,' he wrote, 'but I would rather drive a hearse than walk solemnly about in a red coat after a ball.' He was the first to admit that his indifference to the game constituted an educational defect and lack of good taste, a confession possibly designed as a sop to those addicted to the mashie, the niblick and the spoon. But his apologies were completely negated by his allegation that, whereas golf was 'a puerile, purposeless and preposterous game',[12] croquet was much superior - the kind of affirmation calculated to provoke apoplexy among the votaries of green and fairway! (Quite possibly that was John Kipling's mischievous intention!)

Despite his father's denigration of the royal and ancient game, and backed by the enthusiasm of Conan Doyle for it, Rudyard took up golf and became so keen that, during his Vermont days, he played amid the snows with golf balls which he had dyed in red ink. He continued to play in later life and was to be seen on the links at Muizenberg, South Africa, in the company of his friend, Leander Starr Jameson. He shared his father's opinion that it was a 'fool game' but continued to play because it diverted his mind from the political developments which followed the Boer War. By 1908, in Rudyard's opinion, all the sacrifices made during that conflict had been squandered by Asquith, and he sought relief from political frustration in the pursuit of the wayward golf ball and in the evasion of the voracious bunker.

Although John came to Bombay armed with the highest professional recommendations, he found himself ignored by the Public Works Department. The Governor, Henry Bartle Frere, had inaugurated a series of public buildings in the Victorian-Gothic style and yet, not only was John ignored, but his very designs were pirated; 'each adaptation being worse than the originals,' he grumbled. He deplored the waste of good money on bad ornament and was surprised that a Government School of Art should be excluded from the decoration of government buildings. His appeal did not go unheeded for, in a memorial addressed to Robert Egerton, the Lieutenant Governor of the Punjab in 1882, John was able to claim that 'the sculpture atelier of the Jeejeebhoy School of Art had originated and in a great part carried out the sculptured decoration in marble, stone and plaster of the most important new edifices in Bombay and Poona'.[13]

The Lockwood Kiplings had arrived in India at a time of economic depression, chiefly on account of the cessation of the American Civil War. When it broke out, the blockade of the Southern States had forced the Lancashire manufacturers to turn to India for supplies of raw cotton with the result that Bombay had enjoyed a trade boom. With the end of hostilities in 1865 the 'cotton-bubble' burst; the Bank of Bombay closed its doors; the Governor was recalled to London and censured whilst some of the wealthiest citizens, especially among the Parsee community, faced ruin.

One of the results of this recession was that when Kipling's contract, originally for three years, came due for renewal it was only offered him on the condition that he was prepared to forego the extra fees he had been accustomed to earn by the private coaching of apprentices and students. He accepted the reduced terms but not without pointing out to the authorities that this meant he had to exist on what amounted to a bare subsistence. In spite of private commissions which came his way, he and Alice were condemned to live under the shadow of poverty for a number of years, a state of affairs which prevented either of their clever children from receiving the advantages of a university education. It was a notorious fact that, whilst the higher ranks of the Civil Service lived a life of affluence, the lower ranks were committed to a perpetual struggle to 'make ends meet'.

It was about this time that the European community was both shocked and divided by the outbreak of the Franco-Prussian War. John was frankly anti-Prussian and Francophile. He wrote: 'I don't seem to want many things German, neither her high (and dry) Art, nor her tobacco, nor her cigars, nor anything that is hers!' He described with contempt an appeal issued by the German Consul for subscriptions 'to aid the wounded in the defence of the Fatherland.'[14] Four years later, after the passions generated by war had been cooled, his innate sense of fairness led him to admit that Manchester's pride in her Free Trade Hall concerts was owed to 'some thousands of cultivated Germans' in its midst 'who are really the cause of its artistic superiority to the rest of England'.[15] In thus placating the Germans, could it be that he was to some degree prompted by the ancient feud between the roses of York and Lancaster? He certainly ran the risk of alienating the Mancunian section of the Anglo-Indian community.

The outbreak of the 1870 war had filled John Kipling with a deep sense of horror so that local politics seemed to fade into relative insignificance. He perceived it as a threat to what he regarded as 'the best years of civilisation and peace.' With deep feeling he pictured the rows and rows of wounded soldiers and 'the festering hosts of brave men dead'. He felt the agony of grieving relatives and sorrowed for the great French nation as its studios were turned into hospitals and the thrones, once used by models, into beds. With the eye of a prophet he foresaw that the current trend of events in Europe would reach far into the future: what he did not foresee was that, less than fifty years later, a much greater, world-embracing war would lead to the end of his particular branch of the Kipling family. When, after a brief campaign, Paris was occupied by the triumphant invaders it seemed to John to constitute 'the saddest and most terrible story in the civilised world compared with which his literary activities appeared as trivial'.[16]

In John Kipling there was no fire-eating jingoist nor did he ever engage in the glorification of war. He blamed the politicians for the slaughter. 'We, John Brown, William Schmidt, Jean Crepaud, Luximan Ramjee and Hussein Buksh desire in our ignoble souls to be let alone and to go our way quietly,' he wrote.[17] His expression of such unwarlike opinions cannot have increased his popularity among the higher echelons of either the civil government or the military. Behind his bluff Yorkshire exterior John hid a sensitive spirit, yet he never lacked moral courage nor shrank from the expression of unpopular opinions. When in 1870 the military faction in Bombay had been all in favour of 'going in', John's hope was that they did not mean it. He admitted that there was a strong 'causus belli' against France but, to his regret, he found few ready to share his views.

The most significant events in the story of the Kipling sojourn in Bombay naturally concern the birth of their son on 30 December 1865. It involved Alice in a prolonged and costly labour which was only relieved (according to the servants) by the sacrifice of a goat to Kali, by which means the child's life was ransomed.

Two years later, Alice again found herself pregnant but it was decided that, in view of her earlier experience, it would be better to return to England and put herself in the hands of an English physician. She did this but was once again subjected to a long and painful labour and although her daughter, Trix, survived, the child bore the marks of the forceps on her body for years afterwards.

Two years following the birth of Trix, Alice gave birth to another boy: he was christened John but failed to survive. For a baby to die was relatively commonplace: both Alice's mother and her mother-in-law had undergone the experience: it was a loss more or less taken for granted. In spite of this, Alice received a most tender and understanding letter of sympathy from the poet Algernon Swinburne who had been among the guests at her wedding five years before.

It was in April the following year that the Kiplings travelled to England and committed their children (aged five and three) to Mrs Holloway in

Southsea. John and Alice remained in England for several months and on their return to Bombay found the city infested with a plague of rats.

John's description of the state of affairs vied with Browning's account of the *Pied Piper of Hamelin*. He wrote: 'In the native town they swarm, playing in the streets by moonlight and as boldly as dogs: quarrying their way through most buildings they cry halves with cockroaches and custom-officers on the "nibbleable goods" in the Custom House... they cause half the terrible conflagrations by walking off with lighted lamp-wicks to snug places under the thatch: they run steeple-chases (and carry heavy weights too) on the canvas ceilings overhead and go for their health, via P and O steamers, to Suez and Galle - they always come back: they make their nests in the resonant bowels of the pianoforte - Great rats, small rats, lean rats, brawny rats, brown rats, black rats, grey rats - they are everywhere - and nobody cares.'[18]

The plague of rats led to a demand for improvements in the Bombay drainage system and, when it was opposed on the grounds of expense, John's opinion found expression in his familiar ironic manner: he wrote 'no matter how well-considered the drainage scheme may be, there is an increasing number of eloquent persons who will fight tooth and nail against it and will protest that drains and typhoid are inseparably joined and that the magnificent subterranean system of London and other large cities is a magnificent but deadly mistake'.[19]

Shortly after the return to Bombay came the assassination of Lord Mayo, the Viceroy, in February 1872. He had been on a visit to Port Blair on the Andaman Islands where the British had established a penal settlement. The whole of Bombay was shocked by the violent death of this genial, jovial-looking Irishman though, at the time, the Kiplings had no idea of the change in their fortunes which would result from it.

The assassin came from the north-west corner of India and had killed in fulfilment of a blood feud. Unfortunately, he had perpetrated his crime on the wrong side of the border and became subject to British justice. In view of the circumstances surrounding the killing, the death sentence was commuted to imprisonment 'across the black water' and, although the accused pleaded for the death penalty, rather than transportation, this was refused: he revenged himself by the murder of the Queen's representative.

The Government decided that Lord Mayo's memorial should take the form of an Industrial School of Art to be built in the capital of the Punjab, Lahore. So, through a tragic chain of circumstances, John Kipling was invited to become the first Principal of the new school and, at the same time, the Curator of the Lahore Museum.

After consulting with the Bombay Government and the Secretary of State the offer was accepted and, at last, John found himself 'the master in his own house' and not just of his atelier in the Jeejeebhoy School of Art.

Before he left Bombay John was honoured by being elected a Fellow of the University and a member of the Faculty of Arts, a generous action on the part of the Senate who must have either forgotten (or been prepared to overlook) his jesting comment of a few years earlier. He had written: 'I deeply venerate the force of character displayed in our resolute imposition of the time-honoured forms of England on our Aryan brother. I like to see familiar folk in unfamiliar guise, especially when robes of learned state cover garments of Eastern cut'.[20] This shaft of wit may have cost John an honorary degree from the university: in any event his son was to atone for this deficiency by the collection of a whole hatful of such honours and from the world's premier seats of learning.

In his final Bombay contribution to the *Pioneer,* Kipling took the opportunity to congratulate Colonel Kennedy, the Public Works Secretary, on the construction of a new esplanade along the Back Bay shore, 'a raised walk with a broad and well-laid turf ride.' His Parthian shot was a shaft aimed at 'those snarling little people who drag everything down to ridicule!'[21] Did he not expose himself to the riposte, 'Et tu Brute!': he was no mean hand at the art of ridicule himself!

References Chapter Five

1. *Civil and Military Gazette* 15.12.1891
2. *Oxford History of India*
3. *Pioneer Mail* 20.6.1870
4. Exodus vii,2
5. Joshua x,12
6. KA 1/8
7. *Something of Myself* p.3
8. *Pioneer* 21.7.1871
9. *Pioneer* 30.5.1870
10. *Pioneer* 28.1.1871
11. *Forty Years a Soldier* - George Younghusband
12. *Pioneer* 10.5.1870
13. *Pioneer* 8.8.1870
14. KA 3/11
15. *Pioneer* 16.9.1873
16. *Pioneer* 8.8.1870
17. *Pioneer* 9.3.1875
18. *Pioneer* 31.1.1871
19. *Pioneer* 14.2.1871
20. *Pioneer* 8.8.1870
21. *Pioneer* December 1871
22. *Pioneer* 1.7.1873
23. *Pioneer* 16.1.1871
24. *Pioneer* 16.3.1875

India - Travels and Travelling

Was John Kipling's acknowledged authority on India, its peoples and animals, its culture and religions, gained mainly from the writings of other people or was it the fruit of his own observations? The answer is that it came from both.

Like all scholarly individuals, he was certainly 'a bookish man', a fact confirmed in *Kim* where Rudyard describes the little wooden cubicle, partitioned off from the sculpture-lined gallery of the Lahore Museum, with its heat-split cedar door to which Kim applied his ear. Among the contents of the Curator's office was 'a mound of books', French and German, with photographs and reproductions.[1]

Two of the scholars to whom John Kipling was indebted are named in *Kim*: they are Stanislas-Aignan Julien and Samuel Beal.

For forty years Julien was Professor of Chinese in the Collège de France and, among other works, the author of translations of Taoist texts. Samuel Beal was a Cambridge scholar who, after taking Holy Orders, became a naval chaplain. During service with the China Station he learned Chinese and, on his return to England, he produced a series of works, chiefly relating to Buddhism. In 1869 he wrote *The Travels of Fah-Lian and Sung Yun*. (Presumably the travels of *Fo-Hian and Hwen Thiang* in *Kim*.)

Although no reference is made to other volumes in 'the mound of books', it is fairly certain that John Kipling would be acquainted with Eugène Burnouf's *L'Histoire du Bouddhisme Indien*, whilst his regard for the Parsees would have led him to read Burnouf's *Le Lotus de la Bonne Loi*.

Among English authors, Kipling paid tribute to the work of two Wesleyan missionaries, Robert Spence Hardy and Daniel Gogerly, to whom, in John's own words, was owed, 'nine-tenths of the current information on the great mystery of Buddhism'[2]

He would be familiar with Edwin Arnold's poem *The Light of Asia* which, at the time of its publication (1879), enjoyed considerable popularity.

For a few years Edwin Arnold had been Principal of the Deccan College, Poona. His appointment followed a distinguished career at Oxford where he won the Newdigate Prize. On the strength of his brief sojourn in India he wrote *The Light of Asia*, a rendering in verse of the life of the Buddha and the doctrines of Karma and Nirvana, together with a description of the Indian scene.

On his return to England, Arnold was appointed editor of the *Daily Telegraph*, the newspaper responsible for the despatch of H.M. Stanley in search of David Livingstone. Stanley's reports had drawn from John the criticism that, finding the unvarnished story of his progress rather dull, 'he

6. Indian Head drawn by John Lockwood Kipling *(courtesy of the National Trust)*

invented tales of battle, murder and sudden death to enliven his tale'[3]. The same newspaper was to reject *Plain Tales from the Hills* when first offered to them. A year later it was a best-seller.

At other times Kipling dealt less harshly with 'journalistic embroidery'. In 1877 he had written that journalism is capable of many things and, if invention is occasionally called in, to eke out our halting knowledge, it is usually with the happiest effect.'

Edward Arnold was made a Companion of the Indian Empire following the Delhi Assemblage of 1877, an honour for which John Kipling had to wait ten years. Perhaps he suffered the disadvantage of being an alumnus of the Stoke and Fenton Art School rather than of University College, Oxford. So far as Arnold's work on India was concerned, Kipling withheld comment.

It is evident that much of Kipling's encyclopaedic knowledge of India must have been derived from books - but then, what are books for? At the same time, it must not be inferred that John never moved beyond the confines of his study in his search for knowledge and understanding. Such a situation would have been quite uncharacteristic for, even more than his much-travelled son, John Kipling was afflicted with 'itching feet'. France, Italy, the United States, Canada, South Africa as well as most parts of the United Kingdom, were all places which, at some time or other, he had visited. Indeed, in the Visitor's Book kept at Bateman's, Rudyard has recorded that in October 1904 the Pater stayed four nights 'en route for Athens and Constantinople'; John was then in his sixty-eighth year. He was driven on by an insatiable curiosity and the desire to know and to learn through his personal observation. In the words of his brother-in-law, Frederic Macdonald, 'His curiosity, in the nobler sense of the terms, was alive and active in almost every field of knowledge. All things interested him.'[4]

John's love of travel was confirmed by his American friend, Edward Bok, editor of the *Ladies Home Journal*, with whom he travelled in America following the death of Josephine, Rud's eldest child. Bok commented on what he described as Kipling's 'interesting conversation based on wide travel'. It would have been quite out of character if, during his twenty eight years in the exotic sub-continent of India, with its wealth of artistic and architectural history, its archeological wonders and abundant fauna and flora, John Kipling had not been tempted to leave his study with 'its mound of books' and to focus his penetrating artistic mind on to his surroundings.

What then was the extent of John's travels in India?

It is recorded in the memorial addressed in 1882 to Sir Robert Egerton, Lieutenant Governor of the Punjab, that five years after his arrival in Bombay, John was commissioned by the government to tour the North-West Provinces and to make, for exhibition, a series of sketches of Indian craftsmen. A year later he received a similar commission; this time it was to visit the Deccan to make sketches illustrative of the ancient village system operating there. He made over a hundred drawings, later exhibited in London, Vienna and Philadelphia[5].

During the following year he was to be found admiring 'the rich black soil of the Gujerat' and, with a countryman's eyes, appraising the splendid draught animals - draught bullocks - which he claimed to be 'the equals of the Clydesdale horse and the Suffolk Punch', both in pace and in 'physical tug'.[6]

After a visit to Europe and the Paris Exposition of 1879, he travelled to Bahawalpur in order to report for the *Pioneer Mail* on the installation of the youthful Nawab and to describe his palace. 'Nothing', John wrote, 'could be more European.' The Palace proved to be an amalgam of Italian-style building and Corinthian capitals; columned arcades and cupolas, in some ways reminiscent of the Louvre. The lofty barrel-roofed audience chamber was lighted at one end by a vast lunette-shaped window in stained glass which portrayed a gorgeously arrayed Nawab aiming at a tiger from a howdah. 'The tiger,' John wrote, 'springs like a red-hot poker from the midst of a magnificent profusion of reeds, palm-trees, beaters, dogs and blue skies.' He denounced the palace as 'a twice-cooked piece of classic or gothic architecture and a mistake in a country which possessed two or three indigenous styles of architecture.' It was to avoid errors of this kind, not only in the field of architecture but in all realms of Indian art and craftsmanship, that John always strove as he tried to persuade his students to develop their own art-forms rather than simply to copy European designs.

Nor was it just the architectural absurdities of the Nawab's palace that caught John's eye: he found himself fascinated by the antics of 'a little pug-dog with nose tip-tilted which trotted to and fro along the carpets, unmindful of the pomp and princes and intent only on some mysterious business of his own.'[7]

Among the numerous archeological sites John visited were the famous Rock Temples at Ellora. Sixty in number, these temples had been cut out of remote hill-sides in the Western Ghats and decorated with sculptures. The three main faiths of India, between approximately 800 AD and 1000 AD, Buddhist, Hindu and Jain, were represented. Both the Hindu and Jain temples were decorated with detailed and spectacular carvings whereas those in the Buddhist temples were inclined to be static and contemplative. As Kipling made casts of the sculptures, the artist and craftsman in him must have been thrilled by the work of the craftsmen of a bygone age.

During the winter months John was often summoned to the government headquarters in Calcutta and, in the summer, to Simla, when the Viceroy and his entourage moved there in order to avoid the hot season of the year.

He was also familiar with Allahabad, where the Head Office of the *Pioneer Mail* was located and where he had friends, not only among the proprietors such as George Allen and James Walker, but also Douglas Straight, a judge of the High Court with whom the Kiplings sometimes stayed.

The Kipling vacations were usually taken (as was customary with Anglo-Indians) at one of the several hill stations, one of which was Nassik in the Western Ghats. On at least one occasion they went to Mussoorie, close to the Kashmir border and on others to Dalhousie which, in John's opinion, was 'the most beautiful of the hill stations and the wettest.' His children dubbed it 'Dullhouses' and greatly preferred Simla where life was more exciting (and also more expensive.)

Towards the end of 1876 John made a series of journeys to Calcutta and also to Delhi in connection with the forthcoming Imperial Assemblage which he and Alice attended in January 1877 to hear the Queen proclaimed Empress of India.

It must have been during his visit to the Paris Exposition in 1870 that John first witnessed a performance of the celebrated Can-Can dance, which had so shocked the young artist Rossetti when he first visited Paris in 1849. On his return to India, John attended a country fair and claimed to have seen a performance of what he described as 'that historic dance, as old as the hills'. It was danced by a group of 'purdasi' and, in his opinion, they performed as well as any Parisiennes. It could have been a performance of the Halli-Huk described by Rudyard as 'a religious Can-Can of a most startling kind'.[9]

There was much of India which John had to leave unvisited; much he would certainly have enjoyed seeing but from which he was precluded. Two factors were chiefly responsible for this situation: one was the immensity of the sub-continent: the other, the inadequacies of Indian communications. India was so vast that the people who lived in the southern-most tip of it were as far from the capital city, Delhi, as Athens is from London, whilst to travel from Bombay to Delhi was equal to journeying from London to Madrid. When Walter Roper Lawrence first went to India he was told by an experienced civilian that the more he learned of India the less his knowledge seemed to be.[10]

In these circumstances it was surely better to try to know parts of India well rather than to possess a superficial knowledge of the whole: this John Kipling sought to do. With the aid of what others had come to know of that vast land and recorded in books, he applied himself to learn about India and her people in depth and as far as his circumstances allowed. Within these limitations he appears to have succeeded for Rudyard, after acknowledging his debt to his father in the creation of *Kim*, was able to claim that, so far as the Grand Trunk Road was concerned, he and his father 'knew every step, sight and smell on Kim's road as well as the persons he met.'[11]

As to the inadequacies of communications, the first railway line had only been opened a dozen or so years before John and Alice arrived in Bombay. In the year 1859 there were only two hundred miles of track, but when John retired in 1893, this had been extended to twenty five thousand miles. This extension represented a gigantic feat of engineering considering the great rivers to be bridged, the swamps to be drained and the mountains to be crossed. All this was to be accomplished with the aid of coolie labour, slow labouring ox-carts and hardly any mechanical devices. Even this achievement,

great as it was, represented little more than a scratching of the surface of
the problem of linking one part of India with the rest of it.

It follows that there remained many parts of the land which could only be
reached by road and the forms of transport available were mostly of a
primitive kind.

There were numerous occasions when the Kipling family travelled from
Lahore to Simla, a journey which began by taking the train as far as Ambala
(Umballa). The rest of the journey, about one hundred and twenty miles,
had to be made by road. This was usually by 'tonga' or Deccan dog cart.
When this vehicle replaced the 'ekka', a two-wheeled cart drawn usually by
two lean ponies, John hailed it as a 'step forward in the march of civilisation.'

The journey from Ambala to Simla usually took two days, a halt being
made at Kalka before embarking on a further up-hill haul to Simla. The
time taken for the whole journey from the rail-head varied with the weather
and the traveller's powers of endurance. it was not until 1903, long after the
Kiplings had left India, that a narrow-gauge railway line linking Ambala
with Simla was completed.

Another form of transport provided by the Punjab Government was the
'post-gharrie'. Although often subject to adverse criticism, it found a defender
in John Kipling. In his usual droll fashion he wrote: 'I always want to ride
on the easiest of 'C' springs and on luxuriously-stuffed, green morocco
cushions and drawn by well-matched horses. I dislike dust, I hate the sun; I
like to go as fast as possible'. Whilst admitting that the post-gharrie fell short
of his preferences, he questioned whether any government could do better
than the present one in the circumstances. He asked: 'Are American stages
better?; does the French diligence, the Russian telega, the Irish car or, that
supreme product of English nineteenth century civilisation, the rattling,
frowsy, London four-wheel cab, more nearly meet the critic's views?[12]

Shortly after the Lockwood Kiplings moved from Bombay to Lahore, there
arose F.W. Steven's masterpiece the Bombay Victoria Railway Terminus. It
was built of polychromatic stone from local quarries and decorated with
delightful animal and bird carvings. Some of the Indian craftsmen employed
owed their skills and inspiration to John Lockwood Kipling.

In 1865 the Bombay terminus of the Great Indian Peninsular Railway
consisted, according to John, of no more than 'a squalid and rickety wooden -
shanty.' To enter it, the traveller had first to circumvent 'a crowd of hackney
carriages who refused to keep in line and insisted in charging about as though
their sole aim was to interlock their wheels and set the lean horses fighting.'

Having at last gained the terminus, the next problem was the weighing of
luggage as 'you were almost swept off your feet by an outward current of
hurrying people'.[13]

Once aboard the train, the demands on the passenger's patience and
endurance had only just begun. Journeys were tediously long: the train
stopped at every station, partly because in the early days there were no

corridors and halts had to be made for the sake of the travellers' creature comforts.[14]

During the summer months the carriages could become unbearably hot. According to W.R. Lawrence, 'In hot weather the hottest room of a Turkish Bath was mild compared with the heat of a railway carriage. There was no ice and the water in the lavatory basin would have boiled an egg'.[15]

In order to alleviate these conditions, screens of grass roots known as 'taties' were hung over the windows and regularly soaked with water. Despite this amelioration it was customary to carry a supply of coffins to accommodate the bodies of those who succumbed from heat-exhaustion.

Eventually, it became customary for Europeans to pick up blocks of ice which were stored at the stations and John wondered why the refrigeration processes, which were beginning to be installed on ships, were not employed on the trains. When this was done there were immediate complaints from the people, dubbed by John as 'Indian Salamanders', that the trains were damp and chill and fraught with rheumatism. 'Life,' he wrote, 'is a cheerful arrangement and it is a great privilege to be able to choose between apoplexy and rheumatism.'[16]

What used to annoy both the Indian and European passengers was the practice of the ticket collectors of awakening the sleeping travellers at regular intervals throughout the night with a demand to inspect their tickets. On this account the passengers were robbed of a few hours sleep and an escape from the boredom of, what seemed, interminable journeys. Understandably, this practice provoked 'long and furious debates between travellers and Eurasian ticket collectors.'[17] Even John Kipling, who had a tender regard for the Eurasians, resented those he described as 'the torquemados who, dressed in the uniform of authority, rule the rail.' A man in an official uniform, he observed, 'always wants to bully his brethren.'[18]

Even when the much harrassed traveller reached his destination his troubles and trials were not over: he could expect to find himself 'the helpless prey to a horde of ruffians who are allowed unquestioned access to the stations; who fight for his luggage like Berserks and, in the matter of payment, are insatiable.'[19]

Taking into account the foregoing - the vastness of the country, the immense distances, the lack of means of communication, the primitive forms of transport and the harshness of the climate - the astonishing thing is, not that John Kipling did little travelling but that he contrived to do so much!

John Kipling did not limit his observations to any particular aspect of Indian life: he was interested in the whole spectrum of it. We find him describing not only the Nawab's palace but also the peasant's hovel: he interests himself in the life both of field and factory; in things ancient and modern; in people at work and people at play.

The India of his time was pre-eminently a land of small-holdings and Kipling has described the peasant cultivator and his family as they laboured in the paddy fields 'up to their hips in the fruitful mud'. When the Indian

Mary goes to call the cattle home she seems to him to be 'the most pathetic Arcadian figure one could imagine as she flounders after her wallowing buffaloes, screaming hoarsely against the wind and sweeping rain.' He continues: 'Her limbs are sometimes as smooth and as round as any that Pradier carved but slime covers them and the rain chills them to an unlovely texture of goose-flesh and she sets the muscles of her face so hard against the bitter weather that she acquires the sullen fixity of a wild animal'.[20] John was an artist; his pigments, words!

He saw the peasant girl, not only with the objectivity of an artist but also with the eye of compassion. 'Happily, it is not given to her to know how utterly wretched she is,' he wrote, 'and what a leaky dog-hole is the damp hutch in which she sleeps; how coarse and poor her food, how grim and hard her life.'[21]

Although in 1865 agriculture was the main industry of the Maritime District of Bombay, centred between the Western Ghats and the sea and extending from the city of Bombay as far as Goa, the cotton industry had been established in Bombay neighbourhood for nearly two hundred years and, when the Kiplings first arrived in India, nineteen mills were working there. Just as John had interested himself in the life of the peasant farmer so it was with the mill-worker.

In the mid-nineteenth century conditions of work in the mills of Lancashire and Yorkshire left much to be desired but the 'dark Satanic mills' of Bombay, despite efforts by the government to improve them, were far worse.

The easy-going workers disliked being bound by rules and absenteeism was rampant. The Hindu dislike of the factory-bell reminded John of the song sung by children in the mills of Yorkshire and Lancashire: 'Isn't it a pity and a shame to tell; That all Crawshaw's men should be ruled by a bell.' In his whimsical fashion John observed that the workers showed themselves amenable to discipline, 'when they don't stay away!'[22]

The usual working hours were from six in the morning until six at night with half an hour for dinner and odd times for fragmentary meals taken during this twelve-hour working day.

John admired especially little dark Malwen girls from the Interior, their saris tucked tightly away from their round nude limbs, who trotted around piecing threads so deftly and possessed of a quadromanous characteristic which proved so useful in throstle-spinning, 'where the prehensile toes were used to arrest the spindle while the thread was pieced by hand.'[23]

When a native newspaper warned the European manufacturers that they faced death from starvation, John wrote rather prophetically that 'this is a fearful warning to Manchester and I am not sure that this great city has not some reason for apprehension - Lancashire had better look out'.[24]

As an artist he was interested not only in the economic side of industry, but also in the artistic quality of its products. He approved the patterns used in calico printing and, in his opinion, 'the tone of their work when done on country calico was much better in quality than that of the more mechanically perfect European produced goods'. He also thought the carpets very good, if unnecessarily coarse and large in pattern. Their silks he found admirable in texture, colour and pattern.

During the second half of the nineteenth century the Industrial Revolution was nearing its flood-tide and John Kipling was an interested observer of its invasion of India.

As a craftsman, he had long admired the workmanship displayed in the Peninsular and Orient steamships which plied between India and the home country. 'Floating towns', he called them but he did deplore their tendency to roll as well as to pitch. It was so trying to tender stomachs and not only that; it left 'berth-marks' on tender limbs 'from irritable edges against which they are so rudely pitched!'[25]

His admiration for passenger liners did not extend to the Royal Navy's ship *Abyssinnia*, possibly because she was an American invention. She was a 'monitor' of shallow draught with a steam-driven circular turret and armed with heavy guns. She was able to approach close in-shore and was used to shell coastal installations. John thought that to call her a ship demanded 'a stretch of courtesy' and, in his eyes, she was 'an epicene gorgon'. This adverse opinion did not prevent him from taking an interest in the technicalities involved in her construction, especially the installation of air-conditioning fans and how useful these would prove in liners sailing via Suez and the Red Sea.

Down below he noted that the *Abyssinnia* was driven through twin-screws by engines capable of developing two hundred horse-power and that she was of 1849 tons burthen. So cramped was her accommodation that he was convinced that no seaman should exceed five feet three inches and would need owl-like vision because of the darkness below decks.[26]

Another mechanical contrivance that caught John's eye was Thomson's Road Steamer. It was capable of hauling up to thirty tons and 'thumps along easily and softly at eight miles an hour'; a speed which compared more than favourably with the alternative form of goods transport, the buffalo-cart.

According to his description, Thomson's machine had three fat wheels one of which was used for steering 'rather like a bath-chair.' The india-rubber tyres were some seven inches thick and the real power of the contrivance 'depended on the endless chain of iron shoes in which the tyre is sheathed.'

It was used to haul a train of 'night-soil' carts; also for the transport of heavy materials used by the engineering department of the municipality. Although the road steamer machine had proved a failure in Madras, John discovered that, in Bombay, it could easily haul thirteen wagons and 'perform in one hour what would have taken struggling bullocks and yelling coolies a couple of days to complete'.[27]

Could it be that the Pater's interest in mechanical developments contained the germ of his son's poems *The Secret of the Machines* and *McAndrew's Hymn*?

During the Kiplings' years in Lahore a tramway system was proposed and

The Pater

John found himself viewing the prospect with reservations. The first trams were to be drawn by horses, no doubt supplied by Pathan horse-dealers like Mahbub Ali who travelled with Kim and 'three truck-loads of tram-horses' to Bombay.[28] John's understanding of, and sympathy with, animals led him to predict that horses would eventually be replaced by steam-power, for the strain imposed by constant stopping and starting meant that the poor creatures were worn out within two years. He also believed that not only would the rails prove a hazard to horses, but also that the tram 'would move aside for no one' and would damage other vehicles, not least the humble ekka, 'the chariot of the people.'

Despite his objections, the trams were introduced and proved to be very popular.

References Chapter Six

1. *Kim* p.10
2. *Pioneer* 22.7.1877
3. *Pioneer* 26.6.1876
4. *As a Tale that is Told* - Fred Macdonald p.335
5. KA 3/11
6. *Pioneer* 24.7.1873
7. *Pioneer* 9.11.1879
8. KA 3/19
9. *Plain Tales from the Hills* - *Miss Youghal's Sais*
10. *The India we Served* - W. Roper Lawrence p.229
11. *Something of Myself* p.140
12. *Pioneer* 8.11.1875
13. *Pioneer* 1.7.1873
14. *The India we Served* p.38
15. *The India we Served* p.38
16. *Pioneer* - 12.4.1871
17. *Kim* - Chapter XI and *Pioneer* - 20.11.1875
18. *Pioneer* 26.6.1876
19. *Pioneer* 5.6.1876
20. *Pioneer* 1.8.1870
21. *Pioneer* 1.8.1870
22. *Pioneer* 28.3.1871
23. *Pioneer* 28.3.1871
24. *Pioneer* 7.10.1873
25. *Pioneer* 14.2.1871
26. *Pioneer* 31.1.1871
27. *Pioneer* 21.2.1871
28. *Kim* - Chapter X
29. *As a Tale that is Told* - F.W. Macdonald - p.335

The Family Square

During the first five years that she lived in Bombay, Alice Kipling experienced three pregnancies, all of which must have brought a rueful reminder of her mother's story of the countrywoman who described child-birth as 'a sharp undertaking, Ma'am and the pains of Hell!'

The first of these births almost culminated in the deaths of both mother and child and their lives were only spared (according to the servants) by the offering of the sacrifice of a goat to Kali! The baby was baptised in Bombay Cathedral and named Joseph Rudyard; Joseph in accordance with the Kipling tradition of alternating the name Joseph with that of John, for sons born into the family, and Rudyard, after the Staffordshire lake where his parents had become engaged. In later life, his first Christian name was dropped and he was known only as Rudyard, even though he is supposed to have scorned its romantic associations.

About two years after Rudyard's birth Alice found herself again 'enceinte' and, in view of the hazards she had undergone on that occasion, it was decided that the family should return to England where the birth could be supervised by their old friend, Dr Charles Radcliffe. Their journey to England was by sea to Suez - the Canal was not yet opened - and then by train to Alexandria, followed by sea again possibly on the old s.s. *Ripon*. Ruddy was two and half years old when they arrived in Bewdley on the banks of the Severn, where Alice's parents lived in retirement.

As John looked back on those early journeys, two years later, one of his vivid memories was of 'fifty mother's treasures' who devastated the quarter-deck; tumbled down companion-ways, raced around the saloon, destroyed their parents' peace and imperilled their own lives.'[1] Until that time it seems that Ruddy had been a good, reasonable and obedient child but on the steamer, laden with spoilt children, he became as odious as the rest.

When he arrived in Bewdley he proved himself 'a holy terror' and nearly drove his ailing grandfather to distraction. Reflecting on these experiences, John wrote: 'Thanks to the indolence, and by no means to the indulgence of parents, the Anglo-Indian child is usually "badly in need of a basting" '. He was quoting a Mrs McTeague, the wife of a soldier who was sailing home in charge of the four children of a P and O agent. 'We are willing slaves to our small emperors', John wrote, 'feeling that the best we can give them is but poor compensation for the loss of their birthright of English air'.[2]

Leaving Ruddy in the care of his Aunt Edie, Alice moved from Bewdley to the Grange, Fulham, the home of her sister Georgie, where it was intended the birth should take place. When the Burne-Jones moved from 41 Kensington Square (the site of the Lockwood Kipling marriage breakfast), Georgie had

63

a premonition that something ominous was about to happen there. She didn't have long to wait: Alice was slight in build and the second child weighed in at eleven pounds and cost her mother many hours of labour. When Alice, Trix (as she came to be called) was born on 11 June 1868 she arrived with a black-eye, a broken arm and her little body scarred by the forceps. Even then she was not out of danger: her uncle, Edward Burne-Jones, had wisely absented himself whilst Alice was giving birth; during his absence the child had been born and cradled in an armchair while the mother received attention. On his return the absent-minded artist was about to sit on her but she was saved by a visiting art-dealer; this was her second escape within an hour for when she was delivered it was thought she was dead, and it was only the prescience of Aunt Georgie which led to the baby being picked up, slapped and declared herself alive with a cry!

Having survived such a succession of perils, the new baby was taken to Bewdley, there to be admired by her relations and described as 'a Rubens Baby'. Her small brother heartily concurred with this opinion, for was not Reuben Crowther, the Baldwin's coachman, one of his heroes?

Alice's joy over the birth of her child was somewhat diluted by the discovery that Trix suffered from a cast in one of her eyes. Fortunately, it was only noticeable under particular circumstances but Alice, who had blue eyes and dark lashes, had expected that her children would have the same. Her husband's grey-blue eyes had been described by a member of the Punjab Club as 'beautiful as a woman's'.

When the Kipling family returned to Bombay, Alice seems to have found that, in spite of the presence of her Goanese ayah, the running of her household consisting of possibly six to eight servants, together with the presence of a young baby and a child of three or four years, was rather restrictive. In order to relieve her of some of these responsibilities, John suggested that his sister Hannah should be invited to come out to India and assist with the house-keeping.

Hannah Kipling, at the time unmarried, was remembered by those who knew her as 'a sweet and lovable soul'; even her sister Jane conceded that she was 'a clever woman and a better judge of character than myself'. Hannah demonstrated that she was not only sweet and clever but also sensible by refusing the invitation and, instead of emigrating to Bombay, married her cousin, Joseph Rawling, 'a farmer, though not a very successful one'. It is difficult to see how this homely Yorkshire woman would have fitted into such an alien environment as that of Anglo-Indian society nor how she and her sister-in-law could have lived harmoniously under the same roof.[3]

When Rudyard reached what was regarded as 'the allotted span' of three score years and ten he embarked on that fragmentary biography entitled, *Something of Myself*. Looking back on the Bombay years through the golden haze of time he remembered them as one of the idyllic periods of his life. The picture he gave was of an ideal family in which he enjoyed the affection of parents and the adoration of native servants. He recalled morning walks to the fruit market, his little sister in her perambulator; evening strolls by the seaside amid the palm groves, visits to a Hindu Temple with Meeta, his Hindu bearer and prayers with his Roman Catholic ayah at some wayside shrine. Light, colour, golden and purple fruits, gaily dressed native people; his father's atelier with its smells of paint and oil and the lumps of clay with which he was permitted to play, were still vivid memories.[4]

Sometimes his memory played tricks with him as he wrote. 'Mr Terry' would have certainly resented being dubbed 'my father's assistant' and would have been quick to claim it was the other way round. Nor could his mother have awakened him on her early return from 'a big dinner' caused by the assassination of the Viceroy, Lord Mayo: at the time this tragic event took place both Rud and his sister had left Bombay and were being fostered in Southsea. Heaven may have lain about him in his infancy but now 'shades of the prison-house' had begun to close upon the growing boy.

During the hot season of 1870 Alice once more gave birth - on this occasion to another boy who was christened John. Unfortunately, his life soon ended and it was then that Algernon Swinbourne, the poet, sent Alice a most understanding letter of sympathy.

Early in the year 1871 the Kiplings decided to send Rudyard and his sister Trix home to England; this had become necessary not least because, although he was five years old, Ruddy could neither read nor write. (Trix always wondered what her parents had been doing to allow such a state of affairs to arise.)

But the major reason for the break-up of what Alice had come to call 'the Family Square' was the Indian climate and the diseases which it bred. A hundred years ago this severance of the family-ties was an agony which had to be faced by all Anglo-Indian parents who could afford it.

Apart from the sorrow of parting with their children, the corresponding expense of having them maintained and educated in England must have fallen heavily on the already strained Kipling exchequer. Rudyard came to recognise this fact when he grew up but it is certain that a genuine concern for their children's health prompted Alice and John to take this step.

Fifty years later the Anglo-Indian community were being urged to send their children home before they reached the age of five and Thomas Cashmore, a missionary with the Society for the Propagation of the Gospel, and his wife parted with their eldest when she was only three. It was five years before her parents saw her again, during which time she was brought up by her grandmother.[5] The Kipling experience was not unique.

In 1871 the array of prophylactics with which the traveller is now familiar was not known in India; nor was air-conditioning, unless the punkah and the thermantidote can be so described. As late as 1874 the wife of the Viceroy, Lady Lytton, complained bitterly about the absence in India of the humble water-closet. Not surprisingly, premature death through disease constituted an ever-present threat and it was the recognition of this which prompted the

Kiplings to send their children home. In the Spring of 1871 the family arrived in Littlehampton, Sussex.

John Kipling's description of Littlehampton was far from flattering. According to his account, its shops were few, and largely devoted to the sale 'of antedeluvian novels and evangelical tracts.' It did possess a weekly newspaper which was 'great on the important question as to whether a pest-house should be erected within its parochial bounds or those of an adjoining parish'.

Littlehampton also had a fort where, with the aid of four guns, 'three artillerymen were defending their country'. Unfortunately, the guns could not be fired for fear the fort might collapse so the soldiers spent their days telling each other long yarns about China, Madras and Canada 'whilst the guns looked defiantly out to sea.'[6]

Apart from the shops, the fort and the weekly newspaper, Littlehampton enjoyed the advantage (so far as children are concerned) of a sandy beach and it was there, during the summer that John could have been found superintending the building of a sand-castle.

As might be expected, it was not an ordinary castle but a reproduction of the Tower of London. Its design was based on a plan found in the illustrated edition of Harrison Ainsworth's novel. John found great satisfaction in being able to persuade a number of sun-tanned boys to reproduce, in sand, Cruikshank's veritable plan. The bastion and the donjon were illuminated with candles whilst a small cannon could be fired from the ramparts. The last word (as is ever the case) rested with the remorseless tide which swallowed up the whole wonderful creation. There can be no doubt that John enjoyed the construction of this master-piece as much, if not more, than his young assistants: his gift for entertaining youth was a fore-shadowing of that distant day when his son would hold children, and the not so young, entranced by the tales which he told.

Other entertainments were donkey rides along the beach; a troupe of 'woeful acrobats' who performed 'with only half a chair and no back-bone': there were walks through Arundel Park where, with a professional eye, John watched the masons at work on the Roman Catholic Cathedral then under construction. They played 'elementary cricket' on the common; flew kites and ate 'enormous quantities of bread and butter'. At least once the family even went sea-bathing which indicates a certain hardiness in children newly arrived from 'India's coral strand.'

The chief threat to their contentment was the unpredictable English summer. All through June and July the local people were predicting that 'it would take up presently' but alas, instead of 'taking up', it kept on 'coming down' and it rained heavily. Yet, despite the weather, John was ready to admit, with reservations, that England was the loveliest country in the world. 'Did you ever see Leeds on a cold, dark, wet, day,' he asked his readers 'or journey through that infernal country between Birmingham and Wolverhampton?' (Reminiscent no doubt of his journeys between London and

Burslem via Wolverhampton only a few years before). The Black Country he regarded as 'more lurid in its desolation than anything described by Dante!' He continued, 'Bombay may be madly moist in August but the grace of living nature prevents the torment from being so hideously painful as that of the smoke, fire, filth and barrenness of a leaden, chilly, rainy summer's day in Holbeck or Dudley'.[6]

The weather must have relented because a little later John described how they 'rolled cosily' into Chichester by train and how they spied, on a wayside station, a Sunday school excursion with the young men-teachers clad in shiny frock-coats with flowers in their button-holes, 'conversing discreetly with young lady-teachers in summer muslins'. They passed through sunny corn-fields where the reapers and their reaping machines were busily at work and found accommodation at the Dolphin, opposite the Cathedral.

During their stay in Chichester John was struck by what he called 'the apparent piety' of the place. It contained at least seven churches and ten dissenting chapels. While these were 'all going full blast', as he irreverently put it, he hunted around for a Sunday paper 'wherewith to comfort his secular mind'.

He found the Dolphin an excellent house though lacking 'a coffee room where one might take a lady'. It knew nothing of gas-lighting because the management preferred wax candles in tall silver candle-sticks. He ventured into the Commercial Room in order to smoke his cheroot, only to be ordered out by a member of the commercial traveller fraternity for trespass (not being one of their calling). This led him to the comment that they were governed by a code of observances and ceremonies 'as if framed by a gold-stick-in-waiting'.[7]

It was towards the close of 1871 that the children were finally surrendered to Mrs Rose Holloway, a step for which Alice and John have had to shoulder a considerable load of blame. Their fault, if any, lay in the fact that they failed to take the children into their confidence and prepare them for what lay ahead. The lack of any hint or indication of the separation which was in store must have come as a shattering blow to both Rud and Trix and left a trauma in both their lives, only to be revealed as the years went by. What reasons prompted this apparently callous action have never been discovered: maybe it was that the parents dreaded an emotional scene when the time to say 'goodbye' arrived. We know that whenever John and Alice had to part for a period John became extremely distressed. If it was to spare his feelings, then it was a selfish and blameworthy action. Trix always blamed her mother for what was done and certainly Alice was made of harder and less sensitive material than her husband. Whoever was to blame, the fact cannot be avoided that the course of action, to which the Kiplings committed themselves that Autumn day, was inexcusable. Even if it did not impair the mutual affection characterlstic of the Family Square, there are signs that it left a lasting mark on the impressionable young children who were the innocent victims of it.

Each was invested with a basic insecurity which was to reveal itself in later life.

Alice found foster-parents for her children through an advertisement placed in the *Pioneer*: they were Captain Pryse Agar Holloway and his wife, Rose.

As a midshipman, the Captain had fought at the Battle of Navarino, aboard HMS *Brisk*. Paid off in 1829, he had joined the Merchant Navy and after some years of service was appointed Chief Officer of Coastguards at Portsmouth. When the young Kiplings came to live at 4 Campbell Road, Southsea, he was sixty-one years-of-age. He died three years later.

The Captain's social background was highly respectable. Son of an Oxfordshire gentleman, Mr Benjamin Holloway, of Charlbury, Oxenford, all his credentials must have appeared impeccable. The 'head' of the family was General Sir Thomas Holloway, then living at West Lodge, Havant. Another member of the Holloway family had been a Fellow of New College; another a Colonel in the Army. Little is known of the Captain's wife, Sarah Rose Holloway, except she was at least distantly connected with the Provost of Oriel College, Oxford.

The Southsea house, Lorne Lodge, was situated in a broad road favoured by the professional classes. It was a detached residence with two storeys plus attics and basement. Built some ten years earlier, it stood in Havelock Road which was named after Sir Henry Havelock, famous for his part in the Relief of Lucknow during the Mutiny. Later the name had been changed to honour Sir Colin Campbell, whom Palmerston had made Commander-in-Chief of the Indian Army. The very address must have appealed to Anglo-Indians; Lorne Lodge was certainly not entitled to be called, according to Trix, 'a horrible little house' in Southsea!

One of the advantages the Kipling parents could possibly have had in mind was that there was a school in the vicinity whose curriculum was designed to prepare boys for entry into the Royal Navy, a career which they may have considered for their son; thus, to be boarded with a sea-captain and to attend a Navy-orientated school would seem to have advantages. Later in life their son was to have a 'love-affair' with the Navy and, when visiting his Aunt Georgie at Christmas, he wore a sailor-suit, though this may not have much significance as such gear was commonplace among middle-class children at the time.

Much has been written about the martyrdom inflicted on young Kipling by Aunty Rosa especially following the death of the kindly Captain Holloway. In Miss Plowden's opinion she was well-intentioned towards both the children but in the boy she 'had caught a tartar'. Even his sister admitted that Rud was as spoilt as could be, not a surprising situation for one brought up by gentle Hindu servants who were both devoted and subservient. He had been accustomed to pull the hair of his Goanese ayah, 'without fear even of reproof' and to pelt Chokra, an Indian boy-servant, with his bricks, 'yet he only smiled'. At his Southsea school he scorned some of his school fellows for being the sons of shop-keepers and dubbed a black boy 'hubshi', the Hindu term of contempt for a person of African origin. 'Even the lowly sweeper in Bombay would laugh at a hubshi'.[8] On the whole, Rudyard appears to have been a rather unpleasant boy, so possibly Mrs Holloway is entitled to some degree of sympathy.

What have shocked later generations were the modes of punishment inflicted on this 'difficult' child. One in particular has been singled out for condemnation: the sewing on the back of Rudyard's overcoat of a placard on which was advertised his name and his crime - *Liar!* When his sister bravely set about removing it, she found the cardboard so thick and the thread so strong, that it needed the boy's knife to cut it away. At the time Trix was nine and when Rud sought to dissuade her from this rash action her reply was that, even if Aunty Rosa were to kill her, she would say what she thought about it.

To punish a child by forcing him (or her) to advertise their fault was not uncommon in the nineteenth century.

One of the best known examples is that described by Charles Dickens in *David Copperfield* but Charlotte Brontë provides a further example in Jane Eyre where Jane's friend Helen Burns at 'Lowood Institution' is punished for untidiness by being compelled to wear 'a tall hat' on which was inscribed the word *Slattern.* In real life, George Nathaniel Curzon, Marquess of Kedleston and sometime Viceroy of India, was often punished by his governess in the same fashion: he was made to parade before the gardeners on the family estate and, even before the neighbouring villagers, bearing on his back such inscriptions as *Sneak, Liar* and *Coward.* He had the grace, in later life, to defend his persecutor saying that she was no doubt a good woman and devoted to him, and only inflicted this punishment for his own good. He even claimed to have forgiven Miss Paraman for the misery she had once caused him: what could not be undone was the probable harm inflicted on his character.[10]

Unlike Lord Curzon, Rudyard could never bring himself to forgive Mrs Holloway and in his novel, *The Light that Failed* - also in a short story, *Baa Baa Black Sheep* - and in his fragmentary biography, *Something of Myself,* he displayed a smouldering resentment which accompanied him all his days.

Other signs of 'the Southsea syndrome' could be found in the apparent satisfaction Rudyard was to find in stories about revenge. For instance, in the tale entitled simply *Pig*, Nafferton hounds the man who has swindled him until his life becomes a positive misery. This, in Rudyard's words, is because, 'a Dalesman from beyond Skipton will forgive an injury when the Strid lets a man live' - the Strid is a narrow gorge in the course of the River Wharfe through which the stream hurls itself in compressed rage. Such is its narrowness that, attempting to leap across it, men have been lured to their deaths.[12]

A similar delight in revenge appears in some of the Stalky tales like *The Moral Reformers.* Indeed, the theme of revenge appears in a high proportion of Rudyard's stories.[13]

It would appear that as a child Rudyard was extremely exasperating but this does not excuse the forms of punishment to which he was subjected during the years spent in 'the house of desolation'.

Those years in Southsea present more questions than answers. For instance, why was it that after Rud had escaped to the United Services College at Westward Ho, his sister was left in the care of Mrs Holloway for a further two years; or why was it possible for Rud, at the age of fourteen, to visit the hated place in order to meet his sister? Or how could it be that Alice's family had failed to recognise that all was not well with the children when they visited them at Lorne Lodge? After all, Hannah Macdonald was a shrewd lady of Welsh descent yet, after one visit to Southsea, she wrote to Alice and suggested that Mrs Holloway might be recommended to other Anglo-Indian families with children they wished to send home. She even reported, after another visit, that the children were much improved in manners and attached to Mrs Holloway; that they were much better behaved than they used to be and that Alice could rest assured regarding their welfare.

Another question which has often been asked is why, with so many uncles, aunts and cousins in England, it was necessary to board Rud and Trix out with strangers. Although alternatives may have been considered, it was to Lorne Lodge, Southsea that the little Kiplings came and any blame which attaches to Alice and John is not that they made a bad choice of foster-parents but that they failed to acclimatise their children's minds to the coming separation: to have returned to India without saying goodbye would appear to have been inexcusable. Even if allowances are made for John's fear of an emotional scene on parting - when Alice had to leave him for an extended period, he is supposed to have wept all night - the emotional trauma, born of a sense of desertion, must have left the children with a deep, inner insecurity. Later both sought, in different ways, security in marriage. That Rud found it in Carrie Balestier was to be revealed in the courage with which she faced the tragic events of 1899 which culminated with the death of her first-born, Josephine and also the fortitude with which, sixteen years later, she received the telegram that her only son, John, was missing during the Battle of Loos. With astonishing self-control, she kept the news to herself until her guest, Isobel Bonar, had departed and only then did she take herself off to Great Wigsell to share her sorrow with another friend, Lady Edward Cecil, who had already lost her son George, in the Retreat from Mons.

As for Trix, she seems to have sought security in marriage with a man ten years her senior; a kind of father-figure. Unhappily, in honest John Fleming (according to Alice, 'a model young man with all the virtues'), she failed in her search: thus in the times of her mental illness it was with her father and mother she found refuge. John Fleming, wretched and pessimistic through insomnia would, in John Kipling's words, 'have given a brass monkey depression' - but then he never approved his beloved daughter's choice of a husband!

References Chapter Seven

1. *Pioneer* 9.5.1870
2. *Pioneer* 9.5.1870
2. Told to the author by a descendant
4. *Something of Myself* Chapter I
5. *Plain Tales from the Raj* p.215
6. KA 28/19
7. KA 28/19
8. KA 28/19
9. *The Light that Failed* p.2
10. *Wee Willie Winkie* p.229
11. *Curzon* - L. Mosley p.9 and p.10
12. *Plain Tales from the Hills* p.222
13. KJ. September 1979 - T.L.A. Daintith

Lahore - A City of Twelve Gates

It was in the Spring of 1875 that John and Alice Kipling took up residence at Lahore: a few months later John was comparing it to the New Jerusalem of St John because its ancient walls were 'pierced by twelve gates.' But there, he added, 'the likeness ends!' It proved to be a veritable rabbit-warren of a place; one of 'the most fantastic labyrinths of brick and mortar ever created by the hand of Man.' Its streets looked like deep water-courses, which indeed they were; its alleys were mostly blind and its courts 'a bewildering entanglement'. Prior to its annexation by the British in 1849 it was impossible, said John, to traverse Lahore except by riding on an elephant. The gathered filth of years lay embanked and encrusted on each side of its narrow ways. When the British set about the augean task of cleansing the city their proposals were strongly resented. In Kipling's words, 'The car of progress bore the dead weight of what was regarded as the will of God, against which it was hopeless to rebel. Disease and health both came from Him and nothing that mortals could do would affect that Will in the slightest degree. Inspite of the stench, the words most frequently on the lip of the inhabitants were those attributed to Lord Melbourne, "why can't you let it alone?" '[1]

Today Lahore is a large commercial, railway and political centre with fine modern buildings and gardens but in 1875 it was very different.

Then, the scourge of Lahore was typhoid to which John succumbed, six months after his arrival. From November until the following February he lay at death's door and was only saved through Alice's devoted nursing. His illness caused him to miss the visit of the Prince of Wales and left him, according to his description of himself, 'grey, feeble and fat': he was not yet forty!

The rail journey from Bombay took the Kiplings four days which included a night spent with Douglas Straight, a Judge of the High Court at Allahabad. The Civil Station where they were to live was described by their friend Walter Roper Lawrence in 1879 as being 'as gloomy as its inhabitants were gay'.[2] According to Lawrence 'its roads were lined with dust-laden Tamarisk trees and ugly bungalows which squatted below the level of the road; it was to one of these bungalows in the Mozung Road that John and Alice came and in which they were to live for nearly twenty years.

Their home was by no means luxurious with its impartially white-washed walls, its raw-timbered roof and its doors which never shut properly. Alice was relieved to find that, having been newly built, the place was at least clean and doubtless she intended that it should remain so. The bungalow was also very spacious so that, according to Alice's description, if she wished to move from one of its fourteen rooms to another she had, perforce, to traverse the

72

other thirteen! She also complained that all the dust of the Mozung Road rushed through the house several times a day.

The bungalow stood in a dusty compound devoid of shrubs and plants: this was because the Kiplings believed that shrubberies attracted insects and insects were the source of disease, a theory held by them long before the discoveries of Manson and Ross. In consequence, the bungalow was dubbed by their neighbours 'Bikanir House' after the Great Indian Desert.

It did not take long for the house to respond to the artistic character of its occupants. The dado was lowered to eye-level to the advantage of their pictures; it also mitigated the depressing effect of the empty space above and soon the atmosphere of their home became intimate, friendly and welcoming.

Much of the knowledge regarding the Kipling home in Lahore is owed to a young lady whom John found seated next to him at a dinner given by the Deputy-Commissioner, Captain Nisbett: her name was Editha Plowden. She had come to India to keep house for her brother who held a judicial post in the Punjab Government. This first encounter was the beginning of a life-long friendship and, twenty five years after their deaths, Miss Plowden still referred to the Kiplings with respect and affection.[3]

Like so many of their Anglo-Indian friends and acquaintances, the Plowden family had long associations with India. Walter Chichele Plowden had been British Consul in Abysinnia and was the youngest son of Trevor Chichele Plowden, killed near Gonda, Northern India, by a rebel chieftain whilst serving in the Bengal Civil Service. Trevor Plowden was an Inspector of Police in Assam and when Lord Robert Lytton offered him an under-secretaryship at Calcutta, the gossips had it that his promotion was due to the fact that he had a pretty wife.[4] It was this lady who suffered the embarrassment of splitting her ball-gown down the back whilst making a curtsey in the Lancers. Unfortunately the tear revealed that her only under-garment consisted of a pair of tights. A hundred years later this would have been regarded as a sensible idea, having regard to the oven-hot temperature of an Indian ballroom: at the time it produced gasps of horror from some of the guests.[5] When John Lockwood Kipling heard of the lady's mishap it probably only served to bring a twinkle to his eye.

In later years Rudyard was to pay his tribute to the Plowden family. The opening paragraph of *The Tomb of His Ancestors* runs: 'Some people will tell you that were there but a single loaf of bread in all India it would be divided equally between the Plowdens, the Beadons and the Rivett-Carnacs... which is only one way of saying that certain families have served India, generation after generation, as dolphins follow in line across the open sea'.[6]

It was to John Kipling's regret that the British took so little interest in the ancient city of Lahore and its history and he collaborated with Thomas Henry Thornton in a guide book entitled *Lahore as it was and is*.

The approach to the old city from the railway station lay along the Landa Bazaar, much frequented by horse-dealers and probably the original of the Kashmir Serai patronised in *Kim* by Mahbub Ali, the burly Afghan with the scarlet beard.[7] The Landa Bazaar led to the Delhi Gate whose stifling hot blast almost deterred young Kipling from his nocturnal explorations of the 'City of Dreadful Night'. Visitors within the walls were assailed by such an assortment of evil odours as 'would rob a Bermondsey tanner of his appetite', or so John said. Every house-top was a latrine and the air was heavy with an indescribably sour smell.

It was probably on this account that so few Europeans penetrated beyond the gates and, indeed, when John came to escort Miss Plowden on a guided tour through the city's warren of narrow streets and alleys, he managed to persuade her to light a cigarette in order to ward off the smells. It was considered outrageous for a lady to be caught smoking out of doors and, sure enough, she had just lighted up when a wagonette came round the corner. The passengers consisted of a group of missionaries engaged in a sight-seeing tour. To Miss Plowden's surprise, as soon as they saw she had 'been caught in the act', they burst out laughing; probably, John suspected, on account of their having been advised to do the same. Miss Plowden concluded that, after all, missionaries were human and she was prepared to like them from that day forward.

The Anglican Cathedral in Lahore stood where, in the year 1600 AD, a tomb had been built in which was laid the body of one of the Emperor Akbar's favourites - Anakarli. The girl had been unfortunate in falling in love, not with her lord and master but with his son and, when their liaison was known, she had been entombed alive. After the death of Akbar, his son succeeded him as Emperor and built a shrine which bore the Persian inscription: 'Oh, could I but behold the face of my beloved once more, I would give thanks to God unto the Day of Resurrection'.

The Cathedral was always known as the Anakarli Church (as was the district of Lahore where it stood) and it appealed to John Kipling's sense of irony that both an Anglican Cathedral and part of the capital city of the Punjab should have been named after an unknown concubine.

Before they left Bombay the Kiplings had been assured that it never rained in the Punjab, 'apart from the occasional shower.' Rumour lived up to its reputation and proved itself 'a laying jade' for during their first year in the Punjab the occasional showers tore up the railway lines and 'half-melted the city of Lahore to its pristine mud'. At the same time it almost beggared the Public Works Department. (During one 'occasional shower' seven inches of rain fell within the space of forty eight hours!)

After spending a year in Lahore John wrote 'the weather here is the Alpha and Omega of existence; it runs through everything like a red thread; it encompasses us, inspite of the insidious caresses of the thermantidote, with tight-fitting garments of fire!' He described the climate as the source of discomfort, ennui and mental and moral deterioration; steaming, breathless and heavy with the sense of imminent atmospheric disturbance. 'One rises dizzy and unrefreshed from feverish sleep and staggers out in search of a stray breath of fresh air,' he wrote, adding: 'Even Soloman in all his glory would have found Shalimar very uncomfortable'.[8]

As though the heat, the humidity and 'the stifling hot blast' which assailed Rudyard in the course of his nocturnal exploration of the ancient city were not enough to make the life of a European miserable, to these extremes was added that of the dust-storm described so brilliantly by Rudyard in *False Dawn* from *Plain Tales from the Hills*.

John Kipling's description of such an event was equally vivid. He wrote: 'A dense, fan-like cloud filled the sky and it grew unwontedly dark. Then the wind struck; trees swayed and bent; birds were blown helplessly about and a chaos of whirling dust was upon us; the darkness was worse than anything this side of the Styx,' John went on to describe how people, bound either for home or on their way to a dinner party, arrived dirty and dishevelled: how carriages were driven into ornamental waters or got entangled in fences and when the unfortunate traveller reached home it was to 'sanded soup and gritty cutlets!' This particular storm, which John described in the *Pioneer* of 2 February 1876, was the worst he had ever experienced but 'of course', he added dryly 'there were old Punjab hands who had known worse!'

His experiences of the Punjab climate must have only confirmed the conclusions he had reached some years earlier in Bombay. There he had written: 'I have always held the heterodox opinion that there are certain physical conditions which entirely absolve one from moral responsibility. In England I was inclined to rank intense cold and toothache as the chief of these but, in this country, I have fairly made up my mind that intense heat and the disgusting eruption known as 'prickly heat' have this effect, more decidedly than anything else in the known world. I became de-mentalised more than demoralised under its influence. I parody the pious ejaculation of St Francis of Assissi and firmly give thanks for my sister the sea and my brother the brandy and soda!'[9]

In November 1875, as they approached their first experience of the Punjab winter, he wrote: 'The cold season with its pleasures, pains and penalties may be said to have fairly set in. The mornings are delightful, the evenings, chill and murky with heavy dews; the air laden with the pungent mixture of raw mist and foul-smelling smoke which every right-thinking Punjabi considers the chief delight of this splendid climate.'[10]

By the end of the same month he was forced to admit that the weather was 'as near perfection as can be imagined', but qualified this unwonted praise by saying that it was more agreeable than wholesome, the cynic in him adding 'like most things worth having!'

During the cold season, Miss Plowden became accustomed to spend each Thursday evening with the Kiplings round a blazing log fire. As the ladies worked at their embroidery (in 'true Victorian fashion'), John read to them. His beautiful voice, like his father's, would have charmed the birds off the trees and the ducks off the pond: the dullest editorial became interesting when he read it. It was in the course of these winter evenings that Miss

75

Plowden was introduced to Shakespeare through John's rendering of the Casket Scene from *A Merchant of Venice*; and also through his reading of the courtship of Katherine of France by Henry the Fifth.

Although she had studied art in Paris, Miss Plowden was quite unsophisticated in many ways. When John read the poems of Rossetti and Swinburne she appreciated the words but 'had to get accustomed to the sentiments'. And when Alice sang their friend Rossetti's 'Song of the Bower', - and John told her that the words were addressed to a lost mistress, she had to confess that she had not the faintest idea what he meant.

This unsophisticated young lady was rather shocked when Alice confessed that, before becoming engaged to John, she had broken off an engagement to William Allingham, the poet: she wished that Alice had never been in love with any man except her husband. It is not known whether she ever learned about Alice's other broken romances and if she had, how she reacted!

There is ample evidence to show that John Kipling and Editha Plowden shared a mutual regard but whether this went beyond a deep affection and expressed itself in more than a brotherly/sisterly embrace on meeting and parting, is doubtful. Not that John preferred it that way but Miss Plowden was a lady of strict moral principles. When Alice went to England in 1879 she told Miss Plowden that she and John were to see as much of each other 'as was consistent with propriety' and that is how the relationship remained - however much John may have preferred it otherwise! In 1880 he wrote to Editha admitting that there were times when he could have done with what he called a 'deputy wife' but society was not sufficiently advanced for such an arrangement.[11]

Many years later he wrote telling Miss Plowden that although he had reached the age of three score years and ten, he still mused on old sweethearts, a habit which he found he was unable to give up. 'I muse as I model', he said as he worked in his Tisbury studio.

So far as Editha Plowden was concerned, there is no doubt that she really regarded John with affectionate admiration and, twenty five years after his death, remembered him as 'my kindest friend'.[13] She had continued to take an interest in John's elderly sisters and in John's parents, whom she described as 'Methodists of the finest Wesleyan type'. She wished that John could have lived to see her great-niece, Louie, 'because he was so fond of girls in his gentle fatherly way'.[14]

Not all John's letters to Miss Plowden were couched in flirtatious terms. In 1880 she seems to have passed through some emotional crisis and John wrote in regret that he 'could lend her neither breeze nor oar; compass nor rudder'. The most hopeless thing in life, he felt, was the 'terrible individuality, or rather isolation, of each human maggot'. He wrote: 'I would give more than I possess, to see you in full sail to the haven we all look for. I can only hope that it may all come right but when you say that this is the only plank you cling to I should like gently to protest'.[15]

Although John Kipling was greatly loved by some, and liked by many, he was not without enemies: among the latter was a Jewish gentleman known as Dr Leitner. He had some connection with a local newspaper which he used to snipe at John, attacking not only his work at the School of Art but also his personal character. John replied in kind and when Leitner applied for the law professorship at the Oriental College his comment was: 'If the chairs of Materia Medica or Obstetrics became vacant the ready doctor would kindly officiate in these capacities too!' He continued: 'Dr Leitner is hardly to be judged by the rigid official standards of etiquette or the frigid social canon of Britannic self-restraint and conventional modesty.' Subsequently he had the satisfaction of being able to report ironically that 'the Law Faculty of the Senate had felt that Dr Leitner's self-sacrificing kindness should no longer be trespassed upon and that, since the object of the lectureship was to teach Law, it would be well to appoint a skilled and practical lawyer to the post!'[16]

Perhaps there was a dash of anti-semitism behind these remarks for when Leitner postponed a visit to Europe on account of the anti-Jewish pogroms which were then being practised, Alice's comment was to the effect that she would like to start a pogrom in Lahore and to begin by persecuting Leitner! Fortunately for the Kiplings the doctor suddenly disappeared and was heard of no more.

Another individual who developed a dislike for Kipling was a man called MacDonald. He had been sent from Allahabad by the proprietors to supply during the illness of their editor, Stephen Wheeler. Both MacDonald and his wife received the hospitality of the Kipling home but, when MacDonald became the Simla correspondent to the *Times of India* and the *Indian Daily News*, he used his position to attack some of his former associates in Lahore, including the Kiplings. John he described as 'the laziest and most conceited bore he had ever known' and Alice as 'the sourest and vainest lady this side of Suez.' What so hurt the Kiplings was that they had befriended the man, only to have their kindness thrown in their face.[17]

During their years in the Punjab the Kiplings gained several good and (in some cases) influential friends, one of whom was Walter Roper Lawrence, a young man destined to rise high in government circles and to become the secretary to two Viceroys.

Lawrence had arrived in Bombay in 1879, fresh from Balliol College. It was late in the year and although he had elected to serve under the Punjab Government he had been allowed to arrive there equipped only with tropical clothing. (Apparently English officialdom had no knowledge of the rigours of the winter months in Lahore.)

After an unfortunate experience in a Eurasian-run hotel he moved into the Punjab Club and found himself billeted next door to John Kipling, Alice being in England at the time. In a much quoted passage from Lawrence's book *The India we Served* (written at Rudyard's instigation), he described John Kipling as one of the sweetest characters he had ever known and one who poured his wisdom into Lawrence's callow mind. During the long years of his service to India he and the members of the Kipling family met frequently and he never forgot the general helpfulness they showed him. When Lawrence accompanied the Lieutenant-Governor to Peshawar he was joined by John and they shared a tent. Kipling's purpose in being there was related to some long-outstanding accounts regarding an exhibition in Australia to which the Punjab Government had sent exhibits. He and Lawrence were pleased to be able to boast that a matter which had been under discussion for years was settled within the hour!

When Lawrence was promoted to be the Viceroy's Secretary he accompanied the viceregal entourage on its annual migration from Calcutta to Simla: there he had a small office in the Mall and the friendship, begun in Lahore, was regularly renewed.

Several years afterwards, when Walter Roper Lawrence had become Lord Lansdowne's Secretary, John Kipling was granted a pension by the Indian government and it is believed that his friend Lawrence had a hand in securing it.

After Viceroy Lord Curzon had lost his battle with the Commander-in-Chief, India, and had resigned his post (only to find, to his chagrin, that his resignation had been accepted), it was W.R. Lawrence who saved his chief the final humiliation of having to receive the Prince of Wales, not in the role of Viceroy, but in that of a mere civilian. Lawrence wrote to Lord Knollys at Buckingham Palace and it was arranged that the new Viceroy, Lord Minto, should postpone his arrival in India thus allowing Curzon to receive the Prince and Princess as the reigning Viceroy.[18] Another of the Kipling friends in Lahore was the Lieutenant-Governor, Sir Charles Aitchison. John had performed many services to the Government in addition to the supervision of the Museum and the School of Art. He had also, with the help of his students, decorated the Lieutenant Governor's summer residence in Simla.

Sir Charles was one of those high government officials who had a great sympathy with the people he was called to rule and one who had tried, not only to improve their educational opportunities, but also to open the way to higher appointments in the Civil Service. According to Alice, Sir Charles was at one time unfortunate in his cook for when, in 1883, she and John dined at Government House they were treated to 'a very bad dinner beginning with black soup and ending with grey ices.'[19]

It was to this kindly and humane man that an English lady came seeking advice. As a small child she had been orphaned during the Mutiny and abducted by a Moslem ruler. Placed in his harem, she had been well treated and became his wife. When he died she found herself a wealthy woman. Her problem was, should she acquaint her English relatives with her story or let them go on believing that she had perished at the hands of the mutineers?

Sir Charles said he would consider the matter but, after reflecting on all the implications of this strange story, this kindly man decided it would be best to leave things alone (so great, then, was the prejudice against the marriage of an English woman with an Indian). On the other hand, when the liaison was between an Englishman and an Indian woman (as in the case of *Without Benefit of Clergy,* and *Lispeth*) John's son Rudyard came to regard such situations with compassionate understanding.

Another of the Lahore homes familiar to the Kiplings was that of Captain (later Colonel) Nisbett, the Deputy-Commissioner. It was there that they first met Miss Editha Plowden and it was there that Alice sang 'Phyllis is my only Joy', accompanying herself on the piano which she played 'with a crisp touch'.

When Miss Plowden went down with fever, she was cared for by Mrs Nisbett for, in the absence of trained nursing staff, it was customary for the Anglo-Indian women to nurse one another and for bachelors to be nursed by the men. Alice was accustomed to visit her and when she became convalescent, to take her driving in the Kipling's carriage, known as a Victoria.

On several occasions John used his column in the *Pioneer* to pay tribute to the many services which the people of Lahore received at the hands of the Deputy Commissioner.

It was following a display of fire-works in the Shalimar Gardens that John wrote speculating as to how, amid the multitudinous duties and engagements which the Captain's post involved, he could find the time to organise such entertainments with so much skill and success. 'It is not often', he wrote, 'that one man can so well manage justice and jigs, drainage and dancing, public buildings and public balls, station repairs and station rejoicings!'[20]

It is apparent that Captain Nisbett was not undeserving of the rather fulsome praise heaped on him by John Kipling. Lahore owed its new Court House to him, also the street-lighting (which the young Rudyard on his return to Lahore, could only abuse:) it was, in his eyes, a hazard which invited a man to drive his dog-cart into the central lamp-posts.) It was also Captain Nisbett that the city had to thank for its drainage and water-supply schemes. John Kipling had written, prior to this work, 'the waters of Marah are sweet compared with the nauseous fluids of the wells of Anakarli and Donaldstown, filtered through soil full of human remains, a crowded Golgotha'.[21] Captain Nisbett was also responsible for the planting of trees along the road sides so that the soubriquet 'Dustipore' ceased to be justified.

Shortly before his departure for Simla, the worthy Captain took steps to avert some trouble which was brewing between the Shia and Sunni Moslem sects. Whilst complimenting him on his action, John praised the work he had promoted with regard to the Jumna Mosque which he had restored, not as some newspapers had hinted, 'in the summary whitewash and daub character for which India is famous, but thoroughly with the old work scrupulously preserved in character.'[22]A concern regarding the restoration of old buildings was typical, both of John Kipling and his son. The father had deplored the 'restoration' of French cathedrals and old English churches and when Rudyard visited Lahore to spend Christmas with his parents in 1891, he was horrified to find that the municipal authorities had destroyed the Taksali Gate. This led him to write in the *Civil and Military Gazette:* 'You could have bought bricks from the potter but you will never build a Taksali Gate - full of beautiful light and shade; corners where an idle man could plant his charpoy and dream, niches where the burnished doves sat in the hot hours of the day and the kine of the city used to troop under its arch twice a day making a golden haze of dust without before they plunged into the cool darkness within.'[23]

Apart from dinner-parties and balls, one of the chief centres of social life was the Montgomery Hall. Built in 1875 for the visit of the Prince of Wales, it took its name from a former Lieutenant-Governor, Robert Montgomery, grandfather of the famous soldier of World War II. Although John Kipling admitted that the Hall was one of the finest buildings constructed by the British in India up to that time, certain aspects of it incurred his criticism. In his opinion it was badly lit; its reading rooms were 'models of unsuitability and discomfort';[24] the teak floor, installed to meet the new Victorian craze, roller-skating, left much to be desired even though it bettered the one in Simla - 'both in appearance and shape'.[25]

The sport of 'rinking', John thoroughly approved. 'It had the advantage,' he said 'of bringing you into closer and more intimate contact with the fair sex than any other diversion going'.[26] On the rink he was able to watch pretty girls 'all in a row, graceful and lissom as Diana; swift as Atlanta, and stately matrons, who skim the wooden plain like Camilla' (the famous queen of the Volsci who, according to Vergil, could run over a field of corn without bending the blades and over the sea without wetting her feet). Rinking, said John, is steadily increasing in popularity, a not surprising fact as even the great Mr Gladstone had been seen engaged in the sport on the Tunbridge Wells rink, thereby giving the imprimatur of the Establishment to this new form of recreation.

Watching the gyrations of the skaters as they reared and clattered round the room, John pitied the non-rinkers, the nervous people who 'crept round the side and claimed that it was like being shut up in a stable with all the horses loose.'

The egalitarian in John came out in his approval of the way in which rinking broke through class distinctions. It was one of the few places in India where the clerk and the head of his department, the milliner and the businessman, could meet 'without loss of dignity, on the one hand, or self-respect on the other.' He expressed reservations regarding the proximity of the reading-rooms and the rink as he found reading, to the accompaniment of a 'roaring obligato of roller skates and the staccato bumps of falling bodies', somewhat difficult: furthermore the shouts and screams of the young generation broke the thread of his thought.[27]

Roller-skating was not the only recreation to which the Montgomery Hall was dedicated; almost every night there was dancing and, on occasions, the dance included what John Kipling described as 'an amateur Promenade Concert.' This consisted of 'glees, comic songs and concerted pieces' and was evidently not of a particularly highbrow nature. So far as the main part of the evening was concerned, John wrote: 'we danced like demented Mark Tapleys who were trying to persuade themselves that dancing in a cauldron is rather jolly' and, in his opinion, the concert would have been judged a success in any circumstances but 'in the furnace of the Montgomery Hall at the end of May, it was a triumph.'[28]

He was keenly critical of the particular dances which were popular; in his eyes they lacked originality. Waltzing 'brought down dancing to the level of the meanest capacity' and he mourned the passing of the Redowa, the Mazurka, the Schottische and the Varsoviana. There had been no addition to the terpsichorean repertoire, he grumbled, for twenty years, despite the temporary alleviations of 'the Liverpool Lurch, the Saratoga Slide, the Southsea Cuddle and the Boston Dip'.[29]

Another centre of Lahore social life were the famous Shalimar Gardens which lay between five and six miles east of the city. They were entered by a fine classic 'Arc de triomphe' which, in John's eyes, only lacked an equestrian statue on the top. Though sadly reduced in size and somewhat neglected, the Gardens were still very beautiful.

John Kipling seems to have inherited some of his father's enthusiasm for gardens, although he admitted his preference for strawberries, mulberries and tomatoes rather than for roses and geraniums. He noted that one of the advantages of the Punjab was the facility with which English 'annuals' could be persuaded to grow and that, whilst asparagus failed to flourish, celery did well. The fertility of the Punjab was owed to its possession of five great rivers; hence its name. Small wonder that in *Kim*, Rudyard was to describe India as 'a fair land, a most beautiful land'... adding, 'and the Land of the Five Rivers is fairer than all.'[30]

It was a disappointment to Kipling that, by and large, the English displayed so little interest in the history of Lahore and especially its splendid buildings. All his working life he had been connected with the business of architectural decoration and he admired the various styles of oriental design. One, which he failed to appreciate, was a triumphal arch built to welcome Edward, Prince of Wales, on his visit to Lahore in 1875. It was built of solid brick and a great deal bigger than Temple Bar in London. Also, in John's eyes, it was uglier than most Anglo-Indian architecture. One of his main complaints was the practice of smearing every available bit of wall with whitewash. 'The local authorities would whitewash the Gate of Heaven', he said, 'if they could reach it!' He remembered what happened to Bombay Cathedral when the whitewashing of twenty huge punkahs 'threatened the congregation with snow-blindness!'

One of the few clergy who met with John Kipling's approval was the Lahore chaplain, Mr Tribe (later Canon Tribe). For one thing, he was a good preacher who had won the approval of his congregation: for another he had a concern for social conditions and founded a summer home at Mussoorie for the children of railway employees. 'Education is a great boon,' John wrote, 'but the removal of the children from the heat, misery and discomfort of the plains in the hot weather is an almost equal benefit.'[31]

Whilst serving in Lahore, Chaplain Tribe started an Association for Mutual Diversion, the members of which were expected to make some contribution to the entertainment of the rest. They might sing, recite, play on an instrument or read a paper. In actual practice the more loquacious and exhibitionist members of the association tended to 'hog' the proceedings. Thus, in John's account: 'Although you might fidget, you must wait your turn; even though you are sure that your funny recitation or story is more amusing than Wordsworth's *We are Seven*, if you are wise you will heartily applaud when it is over: this increases your own chance of applause and teaches you charity and loving kindness'.[32]

Canon Tribe also won John's approval for his winning of two classes at the Simla Horse Show; one for the best hill-pony and the other for the fattest animal in the Show!

A somewhat revolutionary idea for increasing the social facilities of the Anglo-Indian community was suggested by Kipling Senior: it consisted of the building of a swimming pool. 'I can imagine few pleasanter ways of spending the last hours of daylight than in a 'grenouillère' of good society taking its ease in the water; floating languidly along or dangling a slippered foot in the clear, cool water; to dive at the approach of a tedious person and reappear at the side of a merry mermaiden would be purely delicious.'[33] Whether or not his fantasies were fulfilled is extremely doubtful: the Anglo-Indian community was scarcely ready to espouse mixed bathing. As for the modern vogue of sun-bathing, the Victorian lady regarded pallor as a mark of gentility and, by means of a broad-brimmed hat and a parasol, took every precaution against the acquisition of that 'sun-tan' which is today so prized.

Before moving to Lahore, Kipling had conceived a similar revolutionary idea for Bombay. In a climate so favourable, 'why not' he asked, 'some form of 'al fresco' night entertainment? A thousand lamps hung in the trees would create a Ranelagh, a Vauxhall or, if he must crown his enormity, a Cremorne! A pleasant garden, a dancing platform, a band and a gaily painted stage would improve the quality of social life,' he suggested 'and why was it so wicked?'[34] There is no doubt he took a puckish delight in outraging the moral sentiments and humbug of the ultra-respectable, a characteristic which he never shed even in old age and retirement: there was always something of the mischievous schoolboy in him.

John refused to use the *Pioneer* as a means to self-advertisement and so there is little about his real work, either in Bombay or Lahore. Whether this was the public-school aversion to bragging or his natural modesty, the fact remains that his columns have to be searched closely to discover any reference to his profession. There are a few accounts of the Lahore Museum and its contents. He mentions 'a Kirghiz tent, composed of felt and a skilful arrangement of willow-rods making it a home for an entire family'. He describes a mace, 'cut out of a single piece of jade, curiously shaped and rudely carved and a fur jacket which any Parisienne might be proud to wear, an itinerant pedlar's stock of jewelry hanging on a stick for convenient display to the longing eyes in the bazaar.'[35] The Museum also had on exhibition what Kipling described as 'a knuckle duster', a weapon which he had always supposed was an American invention. This particular specimen was 'armed with three murderous knobs calculated to disarrange an opponents dice-box', as John believed the sporting fraternity called the human mouth.[36]

The Museum was used for a variety of purposes; one of which consisted of a 'conversazione' given by the Commissioner to which Indian gentlemen were invited. The whole place was brilliantly lit for the occasion and, 'the collections of art, manufacture and raw products were the greatest possible use in furnishing topics of talk'. The Maharajah of Kashmir had presented specimens of the foodstuffs, silks, wools, enamels, silver-ware and copper for which that state was famous. He had also sent examples of painted papier-maché and a pretty geometrical tracery in wood used for ceilings and balconies'. This John regarded as the oldest of Eastern architectural traditions. Finally, according to his report, 'the occasion was improved with energy and success by Mr Baden-Powell.'[37]

As with the Museum, so it was regarding the School of Art; Kipling seems to have shrunk from using his columns in the press to advertise his own particular profession. It was left to Lady Dufferin, on her first visit to Lahore, to admire in the school, 'a row of juvenile carpenters, about eight years of age, learning a trade. They learned carving seated on the floor in oriental fashion and worked away with chisel and hammer on a sort of wooden copy-book using their toes almost as much as their hands.'[38]

References Chapter Eight

1. *Pioneer* 28.7.1876 and 5.6.1876
2. *The India we Served* - W.Roper Lawrence p.20
3. Letters in possession of the author
4. *The Lyttons of India* - M. Lutyens p.98
5. *The Lyttons of India* p.51
6. *The Days Work* - Rudyard Kipling p.102
7. *Kim* Chapter I
8. *Pioneer* 29.5.1876
9. *Pioneer* 13.6.1870
10. *Pioneer* 1.11.1875
11. KA 1/11
12. KA 1/11
13. Letters in possession of the author
14. Letters in possession of the author
15. KA 1/11
16. *Pioneer* 3.7.1876
17. KA 1/11
18. *Curzon* - L. Mosley p.125 and 126
19. KA 1/11
20. *Pioneer* 26.6.1876
21. *Pioneer* 26.6.1876
22. *Pioneer* 5.2.1877
23. *Civil and Military Gazette* 25.12.1891
24. *Mixed Scribbles* 9.12.1877
25. *Mixed Scribbles* 9.12.1877
26. *Mixed Scribbles* 18.11.1877
27. *Mixed Scribbles* 2.1.1881
28. *Pioneer* 29.5.1876
29. *Mixed Scribbles* 2.1.1881
30. *Kim* p.207
31. *Pioneer* 18.11.1876
32. *Pioneer* 18.11.1876
33. *Pioneer* 26.6.1876
34. *Pioneer* 28.3.1871
35. *Mixed Scribbles* 16.12.1877
36. *Mixed Scribbles* 16.12.1877
37. *Mixed Scribbles* 16.12.1877
38. *Our Vice-Regal Life* - Lady Dufferin

The Rulers or 'The Heaven-Born'

John Kipling's generation grew up with the belief that the British nation was destined to rule.

One of his father's colleagues in the Wesleyan ministry was Dr Thomas Bowman Stephenson: politically left of centre, his social conscience led eventually to the founding of what used to be known as The National Children's Home and Orphanage (now simply the National Children's Home, or NCH). Despite his radical leanings, Stephenson firmly believed in the British Empire and its God-given mission on behalf of mankind. Writing in 1882 he said: 'To the thoughtful Englishman it is, next to the Christian religion, the greatest fact of these latter days... men and women of our blood and religion are reproducing good old England all around the globe... there shall be a new world and I believe, in God's purpose, the Anglo-Saxon race is to be a most important factor.'[1]

About the same time John R. Seeley, Regius Professor of Modern History in the University of Cambridge, published his series of lectures entitled 'The Expansion of England'. His theme was that, for the sake of her future greatness, England must take possession of vast territories in Canada, South Africa and Australia where, through development, untold wealth was to be found. Another historian of the same period was James Anthony Froude who urged that if England was to secure a decent quality of life for her swarming industrial population, it must be through the development of a world-wide commonwealth wherein the nation might renew its youth.[2]

It was during this same period that John Ruskin gave his famous lecture as Slade Professor in the University of Oxford, in which he summoned the youth of England to make their country once more 'a royal throne of kings, a sceptred isle, for all the world a source of light, a centre of peace, amidst the cruel and clamorous jealousies of nations'.

Educated as they were in such an atmosphere of thought and idealism, it is not surprising to find that the members of the Indian Civil Service came to regard themselves as, if not 'heaven born' (which was what the native population called them), at least as 'the heaven-sent'. 'They made us believe we have a divine mission', wrote Walter Roper Lawrence; 'we made them believe that they were right'.[3]

One of the Viceroys who ruled India, during John Kipling's years there, was Lord Dufferin, later the Marquis of Dufferin and Ava. Speaking at the Calcutta Durbar of 1887 he said: 'Through the mysterious decrees of Providence the British nation and its rulers have been called upon to undertake the supreme government of a mighty empire (India): to vindicate its honour and to defend its territories and to maintain its authority inviolate; to rule justly and impartially a congeries of communities many of them differing from one another in race, language and religion, social customs and material interests; to provide for the welfare of a population nearly as numerous as that of Europe and representing every type of civilisation known to history![4]

It is quite apparent that John Kipling belonged to a generation which sincerely believed that, if God wanted something done, he sent for an Englishman, or failing him, a Scotsman, a Welsh or an Irishman, provided the latter was of the Protestant faith!

It is certain that Kipling would have entertained reservations regarding the divine origin of the British mission but he clearly agreed that the mission existed. His opinions were based on pragmatic rather than theological grounds. 'Of all the governments since the world began', he wrote, 'it will be difficult to instance one that, more than any others, has consistently striven for this ideal - to do justice and to love righteousness![5]

After he had lived in India for eleven years and had moved from Bombay to the Punjab, he wrote: 'Irrigation and peace have not only immensely increased the population but have changed arid wastes into productive fields and the whole face of the country has been metamorphosed within the last twenty five years.' He heard from those who had known the country twenty five to thirty years before of the way in which peace and prosperity had succeeded disorder and insecurity, and yet how, in a hundred insidious ways, the people are being taught to hate and despise their benefactors.[6]

Among the 'benefits' which the British had conferred on India he numbered the Railways, the Postal and Telegraph systems, the Administration, the Army, the Survey, the Constitution and, not least, in a vast land of hundreds of languages and dialects, the English language which, along with Hindi, was to become the lingua franca of the sub-continent.

John Kipling's young friend Walter Lawrence held similar views regarding the mission of the Indian Civil Service: in his words it consisted of a responsibility 'to secure the welfare of millions; to prevent corruption and tyranny, to fight famine and plague and pestilence and to ensure that every Indian should have the right to enjoy, unmolested, the rites and rules of his religion, his caste and his tribe'.[7] In his eyes the duty of the District Officer was to inspire his staff to seek the above end and to prevent the course of justice being blocked by religious, racial and caste prejudice.[8]

As these ideals were to be carried out by human beings, it follows that the performance often fell short of the ideal: nevertheless, it is quite apparent that the ideal did exist.

Both Kipling and Lawrence were angered by the verbal sniping to which the British Raj was subjected, especially by the Americans. According to Lawrence, it was misunderstanding of the problems confronting the Raj which led to unsound and dangerous opinions across the Atlantic. He felt there was a need for British agents, present in the States, to refute the wild and unchallenged charges of British high-handed tyranny.[9]

John Kipling was more forthright: he contrasted the British rule in India with that of the United States in America. 'If I possessed any rupees I could spare,' he wrote, 'I would prefer to send them to Sitting Bull, Crazy Horse and Old Crow and other warriors of the Sioux, away on the Yellowstone River, who have been half-exterminated by the possibly beneficent but certainly rowdy and murderous civilisation of America.'[10]

He was equally severe with the home-based critics and claimed that it was an English characteristic to crave the humiliation that ought to follow on their being assured that our rule is ruinous to the bodies and souls of our subjects and that we systematically ill-treat and abuse the mild Hindu.[11] He wrote with scorn of the Revd Charles Haddon Spurgeon, describing him as 'the ignorant Jupiter of the Surrey Tabernacle whose modern instances of English cruelties are far out of reach of any knowledge of mine'.[12]

One of the greatest benefits which India received from the British Raj was undoubtedly the railway system. 'The te-rain', in the words of Kim, 'has joined friends and united the anxious'.[13] Not only that, but in time of famine it enabled the produce of more fertile regions to be sent to the relief of the starving. Perhaps above all it was the improvement of means of communication, rail, road and telegraph, which created the requisite conditions for India to become one nation rather than a conglomerate of differing, and often warring states.

Kipling's India was largely employed in agriculture and once again it was the Raj which laid the foundation of improved methods of husbandry and increased fertility. One of the pioneers in this sphere was Sir Edward Buck; Lord Dufferin regarded him as something of a genius. He was a man greatly beloved, kind, modest; a lover of music and sport yet his main interest was Indian agriculture. With this in mind he produced his *Economic Atlas of India*. Unhappily, like so many men of vision, the authorities tended to regard him as a dreamer and starved his projects in experimental agriculture. Maybe he was a dreamer but in his dream he always saw an India 'where two blades of wheat grew instead of one!'

The government made mistakes: one such example still stands on the Calcutta Maidan; the Victoria Memorial Hall, which was built to commemorate the long reign of the Queen. The Indian people had asked for a scheme of technical and scientific education whereby their industry might be regenerated: a wealthy Parsee industrialist, Jamsetji Nusserwanji Tata, had offered a quarter of a million pounds sterling towards such a project but Lord Curzon, who had done much for India, preferred to build the snow-white fabric which arose on the green expanse of the Maidan, described by Curzon as 'the Taj of the Twentieth Century'. In the words of A.G. Gardiner, the Liberal journalist: 'He might have given India an instructed people: he promised it a pretty toy.'[14] And yet it was the same Viceroy who consented to accompany Walter Roper Lawrence on a private tour of the famine and plague affected areas. When the vice-regal progress was accompanied by the usual huge entourage, His Excellency only saw India 'illuminated, white-washed and en fête'. Lord Curzon came away from this tour with an increased

87

respect for the District Officers: 'There is nothing finer in the history of our race,' he said, 'than the determined efforts of these devoted men to save Indians from death by famine and plague, many of whom die at their posts.'[15] It was with such devotion in mind that John Kipling wrote that the critics of the Raj make no mention of 'the horrible hole of the pit from which the country was digged!': he was especially savage in his attacks on those writers who had no contact with the living India: 'tip-toe reaching up with tiny and inept canons of judgement to things they do not understand.'[16]

When, in 1875, the Bishop of Calcutta visited Lahore to consecrate a burial ground for European Christians, John wrote: 'So many Englishmen have died and been buried in all manner of stray places - in the compounds of dak-bungalows, under the shade of peepul trees, in company grounds, in gardens, in many a lonely spot in the jungle and along the lines of the rail their enterprise and skill carried over the land - that it would seem a saving of time and trouble if the episcopal benediction could be spread broadcast at one mighty operation'.[17]

When John's son Rudyard wrote about India he said much about young men 'who lived utterly alone and died from typhoid mostly at the regulation age of twenty two'.[18] Men like Yardley-Orde; or like Scott, who, after eight years' service in the Irrigation Department, was seconded to famine relief in South India, almost lost his life through fever but gained a bride; or devoted young officers who, like Bobby Wick, recalled from Simla-leave on account of cholera among the troops, 'without demur and without question, fast as tonga could fly or pony gallop, returned to their regiments and their batteries as though they were hastening to their weddings.'[19]

The faults of the British Raj were mainly of what may be termed 'a psychological nature'; they were based on the wide-spread view that the people they ruled belonged to a race inferior to their own; the Hindu was a child to be amused and paternally governed. Such presumption, in its turn, led to a shocking display of arrogance on the part of some Anglo-Indians and to a deep-seated resentment on the part of Indians whose sensibilities were outraged. When the artist Valentine Cameron Prinsep came to paint the Indian rulers, who gathered for the Imperial Assemblage, he deplored the behaviour of some of the British army subalterns who made cheap jokes at the expense of the rajahs. In their ignorance they presumed that, being natives, these gentlemen could not speak English (which many of them could) and joked about cutting off their ears in order to steal their jewels. And when the Prince of Wales (later King Edward the Seventh) visited India, he was outraged, too, by the discourtesies shown to Indian princes by some of the British officials and the arrogance generally displayed towards the Indian population by the Anglo-Indian community. Too many British men and women forgot that the Shakespearean plea for the Jews: 'If you prick us, do we not bleed? If you tickle us, do we not laugh - if you poison us do we not die - if you wrong us shall we not revenge?' applied equally to the 'mild' Hindu.[20]

John Kipling was not altogether beyond reproach so far as this matter was concerned. Although he could write wisely that 'much as we love to dwell on its faults it (the Raj) is not altogether despicable and at all events it is the best we've got',[21] it cannot be denied he was a child of his age and of his class and one in whom 'the elements were strangely mixed'. He refused to accept the theory that the British would do better in India if they could 'lose their coolness, self-respect, reserve and frigidity with which we are continually charged'. If the qualities of an English gentleman were replaced by 'the subtleness of Juvenal's Greeks, the superficial expansiveness of the Frenchman, the pseudo-cosmopolitan instinct for knavery and intrigue of a Levantine dragoman', John asked: 'could a race possessing these qualifications be trusted to rule India fairly?'[22] Obviously, he expected that the answer would be, No!

As much as he admired the Civil Service, Kipling found it difficult to resist 'cocking a snook' at bureaucracy and making it the target for his irony. Thus, at the end of the official year in 1873 he wrote: 'For some twelve months I have been your very civil servant and I am not sure that I ought to report on myself on stiff blue foolscap paper, folded and half-margin, embellished with those red-ink milestones of summaries and headings; of paragraphs which look so much more intelligent and wisely concise than has yet been given to mortal man.'[23] A few years later he is to be found suggesting to the Public Works Department in Lahore that they should take lessons in the art of papier-maché, brick-making and use the products to replace 'the mudpie constructions with which the winter rains had played such havoc.'[24]

Whilst always ready to joke at the expense of bureaucracy, both the Kiplings, father and son, held the members of the Indian Civil Service in high respect and showed especial sympathy towards the lower echelons. Whilst the senior officials of the Indian Civil Service were rewarded with generous salaries and pensions, their juniors were poorly paid and were expected to do two men's work for one man's pay; often they enjoyed little respite from toil and, according to Walter Roper Lawrence, they were over-burdened with work, whether in the Secretariat or the Districts. At the same time they were haunted by the spectre of poverty, as furloughs, hill-stations and large staffs of servants (consequent on the Hindu caste system) made inroads into their meagre pay. And all the while, death through typhoid, cholera and fever, or a fall from a horse, took its regular toll.

During the twenty eight years he lived in India, Kipling served under seven Viceroys, at least three of whom had a considerable influence on his career.

When he and Alice first set foot in Bombay the reigning Viceroy was John Lawrence, whose brother, Sir Henry Lawrence, had died during the Mutiny. Two years later Lord Lawrence was succeeded by Richard Southwell Bourke, Sixth Earl of Mayo, whom John described as 'a typical, jovial-looking Irishman whose private exchequer was known to be in a healthy condition and who bore the signs of his nationality so typically that one felt sure he had a shillelagh in his kit and, probably, a fiddle.'[25]

Unfortunately for the Viceroy (but fortuitously for Kipling), Lord Mayo was assassinated whilst on a visit to the penal settlement at Port Blair on the Andaman Islands. As his killer came from the North-West Frontier district, the government decided that there should be a memorial to him in Lahore, the capital of the Punjab and its Dependencies. This was to take the form of an Industrial School of Art. Instead of continuing in the role of a humble instructor in the Jeejeebhoy School of Art, although in sole charge of his atelier, Kipling found himself head of the newly-founded Art School and also curator of the Lahore Central Museum. Being John Kipling, he must have found it ironic that he owed his promotion to a Pathan assassin! After less than a year in his new post, John was summoned to meet the new Viceroy, Lord Robert Lytton, in Simla, in order to discuss with him some of the details relating to an immense project he had been commissioned to carry out; the proclamation of Queen Victoria as Empress of India.

Robert Lytton was Disraeli's appointee and the idea of making the proclamation was politically motivated. It sprang, at least in part, from the rivalry between the British, the Russian and the German nations. Both the latter possessed emperors and as, in the eyes of an Indian ruler, kings and queens were plentiful, the interests of political prestige demanded that Britain should have an empress. Mr Gladstone had disagreed and contended that there was no proof that India wanted an empress: in any case, at the time, only nine provinces were subject to the Viceroy's Supreme Council: nevertheless, Lord Lytton, on his appointment, was instructed to proceed with the proclamation.

Robert Lytton conceived the imaginative idea of calling not just the usual provincial durbar which it was customary for a newly appointed viceroy to hold but an Imperial Assemblage of the Indian princes and rulers from all over the huge sub-continent. Such a gathering could not have been considered but for the extension of the railway system and, indeed, many of the members of a ruler's entourage had their first introduction to the train.

Lord Lytton's aim was not only to increase Britain's political prestige but also to bring about some semblance of unity among the feudal princes, divided by long centuries of internecine strife, religion and language. His hope was that they might find some focal point of unity in a common loyalty to the British Raj. Even the critical *Calcutta Statesman* admitted that to bring about such a gathering would be a remarkable achievement: hitherto it had been regarded as an impossibility.

The particular detail which led Lord Lytton to consult with John Kipling related to his idea of presenting each ruler with a banner, on one side of which were to be embroidered his titles and, on the other side, his coat-of-arms. The problem the Viceroy faced was that, in 1876, India possessed no College of Heralds and hence no recognised armorial bearings. It was the need for a solution to this problem which led him to seek the help of the Curator of the Lahore Museum.

Kipling had a long interest in heraldry and, with the help of his remarkable memory, had retained much of what he had learned: he also possessed in Alice an expert needle-woman. When Lord Lytton outlined his plans, John agreed to employ his knowledge and artistic skill to the production of seventy different banners.

The cutting out of the banners in Chinese satin, later to be embroidered in Indian silk, came under Alice's direction. She had a small army of 'dirzies', or Indian needle-men, and, with only a slight knowledge of the language and without recourse to bribery or threats, the work was completed within the twelve weeks allotted to the task.[27] John's gift for heraldry must have descended to his son, for years afterwards when Max Aitkin was created a peer it was Rudyard who designed his coat-of-arms.[28]

When complete, the banners were to be swung from brass poles with golden cords and tassels: unfortunately, through some error in design (not of John's making), the poles proved to be so heavy that each banner required two brawny Highlanders to carry it and, when borne in procession the banner had to be carried on an elephant!

The Imperial Assemblage met on the first day of January, 1877 on a plain, four miles north-west of the ancient city of Delhi. For weeks two thousand coolies had been employed in levelling the ground and on it were built three structures of painted iron. One was a pavilion for the Viceroy in red and gold; (it reminded John of a Victorian band-stand); another was semi-circular and for use by the Indian princes, the foreign representatives and British officials; the third was for guests and lesser officials. When artist Val Prinsep, commissioned by the Government to paint the Assemblage, saw these structures, he was shocked and said they 'out-did the Crystal Palace in hideousity'.

The Lockwood Kiplings were acquainted with Valentine Prinsep; during the London summer of 1858 - known as the year of the great stink - Prinsep's mother had nursed Alice's brother-in-law, Edward Burne-Jones at the family home, Little Holland House, and probably saved his life. The previous year young Prinsep had worked with Burne-Jones, Morris, Rossetti and others on the decoration of the new Debating Hall (now the Library) of the Oxford Union.

Despite these connections, John Kipling's relationship with Prinsep was not always the happiest. The artist's father, Henry Thoby Prinsep, was a distinguished Indian administrator and it had been expected that his son would follow him into the Indian Civil Service but he wished to become an artist and had entered the studio of G.F. Watts who rented rooms at Little Holland House.

In the opinion of Editha Plowden, Prinsep 'used' John and, whilst happy to accept from him help and guidance, was in the habit of disparaging his art teachers, both in Burslem and South Kensington. Despite these frictions, John's inherent generosity led him to write appreciatively of Prinsep's work during his stay in India. He described his picture of the Assemblage as being 'monumental in its completeness'; he also expressed the hope that Mr Prinsep's visit would lead to a more careful consideration of Indian schools of art.

The enormous task of working the banners left Alice in a state of nervous and physical exhaustion. Shortly before commencing the task she had spent some months nursing John after he had nearly succumbed to typhoid fever. As a result, her usually sanguine nature deserted her and she became depressed. Perhaps she found some consolation by reflecting on her first introduction to the new Viceroy: when he had expressed surprise at meeting Burne-Jones' sister-in-law out in India, her response had been to the effect that she also had been surprised to meet Owen Meredith there (the pseudonymn under which Lord Lytton wrote poetry) and when the Viceroy saw his personal banner, with its supporting angels embroidered by Alice, he described her work as 'Angels, wrought by an Angel'.

The Durbar Street and Tent were lit by gas, produced from castor oil, the triple cast-iron lamps being to John Kipling's designs. For this work and also the design of the banners, John's reward was 500 rupees and a silver medal which Alice considered quite inadequate. On the other hand he gained considerably in prestige.

The responsibility for transport for the guests to the place of the Assemblage was in the hands of the travel agents, Thomas Cook and when, in 1886, they were invited to arrange pilgrimages to Mecca, Mr J.M. Cook (son of the founder of the firm) sent his son, Frank H. Cook, to make the arrangements. Among his contacts was John Kipling. His instructions ran: 'Of course you will introduce yourself to Mr Kipling, the Head of the School of Art - his son is the Manager or Editor of the chief newspaper of that district, the *Civil and Military Gazette*.[30] Evidently John Kipling's reputation was already established, though not his son's! The relationship with Thomas Cook's, begun by the father, was in later years to prove most beneficial to his son. When, in the course of his honeymoon, Rudyard and his bride arrived in Yokohama only to discover that the Oriental Banking Company had closed its doors and suspended payment, Cook's refunded the fares and the Canadian Pacific Railway transported them back across Canada free of charge (no doubt at Cook's instigation).[31]

Again, in 1913, Rudyard and his wife were returning from a visit to Egypt and motoring across France. On arrival at Bourges, he learned that the King of Greece was to be buried the following Sunday 'and it behoved me to get down there in time for the affair'. Once more Thomas Cook and Son came to the rescue: they discovered that the funeral had been postponed until the following Wednesday (something it seems Reuters did not know) and, at the same time, supplied Rudyard with two possible rail/steamer combinations which would have enabled him to arrive in Athens in time for the ceremony. In the event, another reporter was sent and found the information 'tremendously useful'.[32] Rudyard probably enjoyed relating this story, to his friend Sir Roderick Jones, Chairman of Reuters!

Lord Robert Lytton's successor as Viceroy was George Frederick Samuel

Robinson, son of the first Earl of Ripon. He had been 'born in the purple' at No. 10 Downing Street during the year his father was a somewhat inept Prime Minister. Following his father into politics, he quickly rose to eminence and in 1866 was made Secretary of State for India. In 1880 Mr Gladstone appointed him Viceroy of India and charged him with the task of preparing the way for eventual self-government by the Indian people. One of the means by which this was to be implemented was the Ilbert Bill, under whose clauses Indian magistrates and judges were to be allowed to preside over courts where British and Europeans appeared as defendants.

The prospect of losing their privilege of being tried only by European judges so enraged the Anglo-Indians that political feelings boiled over: some even went so far as to boycott Vice-regal levies.

John Kipling's sympathies seem to have been with his fellow-countrymen for he wrote to Miss Plowden saying that if Lord Dufferin had not come to replace Lord Ripon, 'poor Anglo-India would have gone crazy with vexation and apprehension'.[33] It seems that the British Government had been compelled to send one of their 'ace negotiators' and Kipling had every confidence in the new man. Thirty years after, when Wilfrid Blunt invited 'old Kipling' to visit him at Newbuildings Place, Sussex, in order to discuss the Morley-Minto Reforms, he was disappointed to find that his political opinions were still those of a typical Anglo-Indian.

A few months after his arrival in India, Lord Ripon made the usual Vice-regal Progress to the Punjab and Kipling had 'to work like a negro slave' on the decorations for the Lahore Ball.

Unfortunately, Alice was ill and he was unable to attend. He did, however, meet the Viceroy for, writing to Miss Plowden, he gave a rather unkind description of 'the new man's discovery of India.' He wrote: 'People stood about helpless and hopeless as he gushed and drivelled.[34] At the same time he was prepared to like Lord Ripon and, when it was complained that his lordship was far too good-humoured, and great peril could come to the State from his good nature, Kipling defended him. 'Are we to distrust the new pilot because he is cheerful?' he asked.[35]

Many years afterwards, Rudyard visited Lord Ripon's Yorkshire estates of Studley Royal and Fountains Abbey and pronounced the early seventeenth century Fountains Hall as being 'a perfect gem of its kind'.[36]

The 'new man' who followed Lord Ripon was Frederick Temple Hamilton-Temple Blackwood, the cultured product of Eton and Oxford; a distinguished diplomat who had been rewarded for his services, in respect of Irish affairs, with the Royal permission to revive the ancient earldom of Dufferin and Clandeboye.

Prior to his appointment as Viceroy of India, Lord Dufferin had held the post of Deputy-Governor-General of Canada: he had also been British Ambassador at St Petersburg, Constantinople, Rome and Paris. He had the reputation of being the possessor of a quick Irish wit and a shrewd mind. His unfailing courtesy was such that it gave the impression of being affected (which it was not). He lisped and wore the fashionable monocle. The superficial impression he created was that of being a character out of a P.G. Wodehouse novel: it was quite a false one. Lord Dufferin was always eager for Constitutional advance on the part of the Indian people: it was during his viceroyship that the National Congress first met at Poona.

The historian W.H. Lecky (never inclined to over-praise) in a speech given in 1902 in honour of Lord Roberts, referred to the former Viceroy as 'a great diplomat and statesman possessed of qualities of brilliance and charm and unequalled tact; a rare sagacity of judgement and a tenacious will'.[37] To all these qualities Lecky might well have added that of magnanimity. It was this virtue of magnanimity which enabled the friendship between the Dufferin family and the Kiplings to continue well after His Excellency had left India. A certain coolness had developed between the two families on account of the infatuation which Lord Dufferin's eldest son had developed for John Kipling's daughter, Trix. If her account is to be believed, Viscount Clandeboye proposed marriage on two occasions but she had refused him, much to the relief no doubt of both sets of parents!

The situation cannot have been helped by the gossip regarding the Viceroy and Alice Kipling, with whom he became accustomed to take tea and whose wit had led him to declare that dullness and Mrs Kipling were never to be found in the same room. Reflecting on those Simla days, he concluded that although the life of a viceroy was a lonely one it was better to keep at a distance 'the pretty women who might condescend to cheer him'.[38]

The first contact made by members of the Kipling family with the new Viceroy may well have come about during the Spring of 1885 when Lord Dufferin visited the Punjab and achieved his first diplomatic success in India through his meeting with the Amir of Afghanistan, only recently hostile. Rudyard described the occasion in the last story of the first *Jungle Book* which begins: 'It rained heavily for one whole month, raining on a camp of thirty thousand men, thousands of camels, elephants, horses, bullocks and mules all gathered together at a place called Rawal Pindi (*sic*) to be reviewed by the Viceroy of India.'[39]

When His Excellency moved down to Lahore, Lady Dufferin's memoirs indicate that they visited the Museum and the Mayo Industrial School of Art. This may well have been the first meeting of 'the Keeper of the Wonder House' and the new Viceroy, although the Vicereine made no mention of John Kipling; only of some of his pupils engaged in learning a trade.[40] It was during the next Simla season, when the Viceroy, the Commander-in-Chief, the Lieutenant Governor of the Punjab and their respective entourages moved to Simla, that the friendship with Lord Dufferin and various members of his family began.

The effect of this élite connection, so far as the Kiplings were concerned, was 'to open doors': the Viceroy had them put on the Government House 'Free List': Lord Roberts, the Commander-in-Chief followed suit and the results were not unnaturally, what Trix described as 'many pleasant invitations'.

On New Year's Day, 1887, John was granted the dignity of a Companion of the Order of the Indian Empire, an Order instituted at the time of the Imperial Assemblage of 1877.

Lord Dufferin was succeeded by Henry Charles Keith Petty Fitzmaurice, Lord Lansdowne, like his predecessor, a product of Eton and Oxford. During his vice-royalty his Private Secretary was John Kipling's young friend Walter Roper Lawrence, and it was Lord Lansdowne who secured for John the government pension which enabled him to retire, before India had devoured both him and Alice. Various people have been given the credit for this welcome concession but we have it on the authority of Rud's wife, Carrie, that it was during Lord Lansdowne's viceroyship that it was conceded.[41] On 16 June that year Rud met his father in New York and, with the help of his friend, Lockwood de Forest, persuaded John to accept retirement. There is no doubt that the Dufferin connection must have helped but it can be assumed that the Viceroy's Secretary, Walter Roper Lawrence, seized the opportunity to repay some of the kindnesses received from his old friend at a time when he most needed help and guidance.

References Chapter Nine

1. *A Man for All Children* - C.J. Davey p.96
2. *Oceana* - J.A. Froude
3. *The India we Served* - W. Roper Lawrence p.43
4. *Life of Lord Dufferin* - A.C. Lyall p.158
5. *Pioneer* 27.6.1870
6. *Pioneer* 17.7.1876 and 31.7.1876
7. *The India we Served* p.112
8. *The India we Served* p.113
9. *The India we Served* p.225
10. *Pioneer* 11.12.1876
11. *Pioneer* 26.7.1870
12. *Pioneer* 27.6.1870
13. *Kim* p.282
14. *Prophet, Priest and Kings* - A.G. Gardiner p.222
15. *The India we Served* p.228
16. *Beast and Man* p.247
17. *Pioneer* 1.11.1875
18. *Something of Myself* p.41
19. *Only a Subaltern - Days Work* p.90
20. *Merchant of Venice*, iii,i
21. *Pioneer* 31.7.1876
22. *Pioneer* 31.7.1876
23. *Pioneer* 21.3.1871
24. *Pioneer* 29.5.1876
25. *Beast and Man* p.104
26. KA 1/9
27. KA 3/19
28. *Beaverbrook* - A.J.P. Taylor p.127
29. *Pioneer* 1.5.1877
30. Thomas Cook Archive
31. *The Strange Ride* - A. Wilson p.180
32. Letter to Thos Cook 1.4.1913
33. KA 1/11
34. KA 1/9
35. *Something of Myself* p.50
36. KA 1/11
37. *Life of Lord Dufferin* - A.C. Lyall ii-150
38. *Life of Lord Dufferin* - A.C. Lyall ii-22
39. *Jungle Book* p.249
40. *Life of Lord Dufferin* - A.C. Lyall ii-117
41. Diaries 27.2.1893

The Soldiers

It used to be said that India was ruled by about a thousand civil servants backed up by half the British Army, yet the truth is, India was governed by relatively few civil servants and a relatively small force of troops. In 1857, at the time of the Mutiny, there were less than forty thousand British soldiers stationed in India, a force that was increased to fifty thousand when the total strength of the Regular Army was 178,000.

John Kipling's contacts with the Indian Army may well have begun when he originated and, in great part, carried out work on the sculptural decoration, in marble, stone and plaster of the new public buildings in Poona.[1] These were the hot-weather headquarters of the Governor of Bombay and a considerable cantonment was situated there.

In the same year that John was appointed Bombay Correspondent to the *Pioneer*, Charles George Gordon, a divisional commander in Poona (and later 'Gordon of Khartoum') was suspended. In Kipling's opinion the reason was Gordon's resentment of what he regarded as interference with the privileges of his rank: John's comment was that 'in default of the proverbial woman there was a member of what Sidney Smith called "the third sex" ' involved. When, about two months later, Gordon was removed from his post Kipling described this as 'a triumph for the Bombay Commander-in-Chief and for the influential persons who so warmly espoused his quarrel.' When Gordon returned to England he added: 'It is confidently believed that the first suspended, and then removed, officer will be righted and set on his feet at home'.[2] John Lockwood Kipling was no respecter of persons, military or otherwise!

In 1880, Gordon was appointed Military Secretary to a new Viceroy, Lord Ripon. Before leaving for India, Gordon called on Wilfrid Scawen Blunt in London who described him as a 'quiet, unmilitary little man with grey eyes and greying hair behind which lay a mind and conscience incapable of compromise. Gordon arrived in Bombay already prejudiced against the Raj, having told Blunt that British vested interests (and not least the Indian Civil Service) made the chances of reform slight.[3]

On his arrival in Bombay, the new Viceroy received a poem from a Parsee and Gordon was instructed to acknowledge it, saying that Lord Ripon had read it with pleasure and interest. As His Excellency had done nothing of the sort, Gordon (being Gordon) refused and had no option but to resign. His successor as Military Secretary was Lord William Beresford who held the post under the next three viceroys. The brother of the Marquis of Waterford and son of a military family, whose record of service stretched back to Wellington's Peninsular campaigns, he became a popular figure in the Anglo-Indian community and an acquaintance of the Kiplings.

It was John Kipling's wide-ranging knowledge which brought him into contact with two other military figures, Robert Baden-Powell, a subaltern in the 13th Hussars, and Arthur, Duke of Connaught, who had commanded a Brigade of Guards at Tel el Kebir before being given the Bombay command. The Queen's diary, dated 22 August 1890, confirms that her son Arthur 'knew Mr Lockwood Kipling well'. This acquaintance could well have been cultivated by the Duke's interest in collecting Indian brass-ware.

When John complimented Baden-Powell on being an authority on the manufactures and products of the Punjab, he can scarcely have imagined that this young officer would attain international fame as the founder of a world-wide movement for boys, nor that the movement would be linked with books of animal stories (*The Jungle Books*), which Rudyard would write and with which John co-operated, although he rejected any mention of the part he was to play in their writing.

The Commander-in-Chief in India from 1885-1893 was Sir Frederick Roberts, later Lord Roberts of Kandahar, Pretoria and Waterford. Born in Cawnpore, he had passed through Eton and Sandhurst and, after training as an East-India cadet at Addiscombe, had joined the Bengal Artillery. Six years later he had been caught up in the Mutiny of 1857, during which he gained the Victoria Cross. Because of his small stature he was known affectionately as 'Little Bobs'. In 1880 he had defeated and dispersed the troops of Yakoub Khan before Kabul and avenged the massacre at the British residency which had occurred earlier in that year. From Kabul he made his famous march on Kandahar and was rewarded with a barony.

After his appointment as Commander-in-Chief, Roberts used to reside at Snowden, a castellated mansion at the opposite end of Simla from Peterhof, the vice-regal residence. Amateur theatrical performances were held there in which members of the Kipling family shared but the proudest moment of Rudyard's young life came when he rode up the Mall side by side with Roberts - a little red-faced man on a fiery chestnut - 'while he asked me what the men thought about their accommodation, entertainment rooms and the like.'[4] This acquaintance was to continue through the years and when, in 1914, John Kipling's grandson (also John) was turned down by the army on account of his eyesight, it was to Lord Roberts that Rudyard turned and through him that young John was commissioned in the Irish Guards, thus leading to his death in France when just past his eighteenth birthday: it also led to the end of that particular branch of the Kipling family.

Although the Kiplings became closely associated with what Rudyard called 'the hierarchy', his father had long shown an interest in the lot of the ordinary soldier and a concern for his welfare. Life in the ranks was 'not a happy one', exposed as the men were, not only to the enemy, when skirmishing on the Frontier, but also to the rigours of the climate and the onslaught of disease. In the columns of the *Pioneer* John often championed their cause.

Whilst he was averse to drunkenness, whether on the part of soldier, sailor or civilian, his approach to the problem was essentially practical. He accepted the fact that the soldier will come by his liquor despite rules and regulations and deplored the exploitation which frequently caused him 'to pay the price of a bottle of best French brandy for a bottle of vile native spirits, dear at six annas!'

The sight of the British soldier 'on the spree' moved him more to pity than disgust and brought from him the plea that better provision should be made for the men's needs. It was with a young soldier in mind, 'with a pleasant boyish face disfigured by drink, bragging of the vengeance he would wreak for being robbed of two rupees', that John advocated the provision of a place 'where drinking to excess would not be forced on a decent man and where wholesome food and drink could be obtained'.[5]

A few weeks later John was able to report that a concert party (then called a Nigger Minstrel Troupe) from the troop-ship *Malabar* had raised four hundred rupees towards the building of a 'Stranger's Home'. On the other hand, he deplored the attempt on the part of 'the hierarchy' to close the bar in the Bombay Sailor's Home. In John's opinion such an action was designed to send the sailor to less wholesome sources. As in the case of General Gordon, so with that of the common sailor and soldier, Kipling was not afraid to challenge the hierarchy and wrote bitterly about 'those ladies and gentlemen who enjoy a drink in clubs and houses any hour of the day or night, but deny the poor soldier a drop'. He agreed that taken in excess, strong drink did much harm but asked 'how many of his readers abstained from strong drinks because some abuse them'.

In like fashion John's son was to protest against 'the official virtue' which decreed that the bazaar prostitutes should not be medically inspected, nor the men taught elementary precautions in their dealings with them, a ruling which cost the Indian Army nine thousand casualties a year laid up with venereal disease. And when Lord Roberts failed to oppose the closing down of licensed brothels throughout India, Rud accused him of imposing a 'chapel-made absurdity' on the soldiers.[6] He plainly shared the Pater's sympathy with the common soldier and his lot.

Originally, the British garrison at Lahore had been stationed at Anakarli but such were the inroads made by disease that a huge cantonment was built at Mean Mir, well outside the city. It was situated on what John described as 'a desert swept by the winds... a desolation of dryness devoid of vegetation'. Ironically, he wrote: 'so ghastly did I find it in its bleak ugliness that it seemed as if it must be wholesome!'[7] Its streets were planned on what he called 'Brobdingnagian' style, broad as boulevards, bare as billiard tables, its houses separated by leagues of dust.' Some years earlier he had approved the introduction of asphalt as being easier to lay than tiles, restricting the dust which, in his opinion, was a cause of opthalmia among the troops.[8]

Despite the fact that in their grim austerity the new barracks seemed to defy pestilence, it was still liable to be ravaged by cholera which had no more respect for the long lines of barracks than for the dirty slums of a crowded city: during a single epidemic there were three hundred casualties among the Royal Scots, a catastrophe which caused Kipling to urge the authorities to provide proper drainage and a clean water supply both of which were lacking.[9] Before it was established that cholera was both air and water-borne, John Kipling suspected the latter as a means of infection.

The interest which John Kipling and his family displayed in the theatre both in Bombay and Lahore took them to the cantonment at Mean Mir where the 63rd West Suffolks were performing what John described as 'a grand melodrama in five acts'. Somewhat condescendingly he wrote in the *Pioneer*: 'Opinions are undecided as to the plot but most of the characters were killed and made long speeches as they lay dying.'[10]

The presence of the Army in the Punjab and on the North-West Frontier received John's full approval. The year following his arrival in Lahore he travelled to Rawalpindi which he described as 'that military hot-house, chokeful of soldiers, parading and marching and beating the drum, individually perhaps rather bored but collectively exerting a salutory moral influence.'[11] It was during the Kipling's years in Lahore that evidence was found that, not only were the Russians supplying arms to the Afghan armies, but there was a serious conspiracy against the peace and security of the Indian Empire. After the defeat at Kabul, Yakub Khan had confessed to a secret treaty, the last clause of which contained a promise by Russia to restore 'the ancient country of Afghanistan': this meant the Peshawar Valley and the Upper Punjab.

After the durbar at Rawalpindi in 1880, John pictured the return of the marching regiments 'to the hills or the distant cantonments in the plains, or to England, where the kilted warriors of the 92nd Regiment (the Gay Gordons) will be striding down Princes Street, climbing the Calton Hill and telling their adventures to sympathetic Edinburgh lasses'.[12] It was a peculiar quirk of John's character that, despite having married a Macdonald, he never seemed to grasp that Scotland was not just another English county like his native Yorkshire.

The responsibility of the troops stationed around Lahore was the policing of the North-West Territories and, in 1877, John reported that a small tribe of Afridis, known as the Jowakis, had been guilty of a series of outrages around Khelat. In response a force led by General Keyes had compelled them to restore stolen property, including British weapons and to surrender the leaders of an attack on an infantry camp: then the country was to be surveyed and a military road built.

A further military responsibility was the protection of travellers and survey parties - in Kipling's opinion 'a one-sided business which the British soldier cannot fairly be expected to win'. On the other hand, 'the half-patriotic brigand can look forward to 'a pension, a Delhi medal and ending his days as a peaceful constable.' He also foresaw the days when these Rob Roy figures would 'make excellent subjects for the inventive writer of picturesque fiction', little imagining that his own son would be one of them.

In the meantime the only effective policy in John's mind was that of continued repression. 'Barbarous themselves,' he wrote, 'they can only be moved by barbarous measures; bloodshed and spoilation are cruel and inhuman but they will have no other. Nor would it be difficult to show that the forebearance displayed of late has emboldened them to pursue the turbulent course which led to the last expedition. Leniency would be a mistake: Afridi logic is simple: incapable themselves of forebearance or forgiveness the only explanation they can find for these qualities is weakness and cowardice.'[13] It was this kind of thinking, no doubt widely held a hundred years ago, which sent a force of Ghurkas, Sikhs, Punjab Cavalry, a mountain-battery and a contingent of the Guides to compel reparations. To the home-based humanitarians, as Kipling called them, who urged that the British should abandon the horrible practice of killing Afridis, his reply was: 'By all means - but let our friends the murderers, set the example.' He agreed it was a thousand pities that expeditions of the kind he had described should be necessary but, in his eyes, they were akin to the pacifying legions of Caesar, and he condemned those critics to whom 'fresh conquest was more distasteful than defeat and disaster'.

There is no doubt that in the 1870s Kipling could have produced plenty of examples which justified his opinions. Travellers to Peshawar were accus-tomed to keep a revolver under the mattress on which they lay in the dak-gharri, a practice which John described as not being of the slightest use. 'The Afridi', he said, 'stayed hidden behind a stone taking leisurely pot-shots, very often with a high-class breech-loading rifle.' Once he felt he had enjoyed sufficient target practice, he would fade into the hills and it was only when the traveller reached Peshawar he would have the oportunity to study the various types of rascality to be met there. Some of them John thought very handsome and well-built. Furthermore, he added, the visitor might also be greatly edified by the sight of the Khyber Pass 'where we Lords of Conquest must not venture to pass on any account.'[14] This ironic comment seems to have been quite lost on John's son for, while in Peshawar, he took the opportunity to travel as far as the mouth of the Khyber where he believed he came under fire from the Afridis and could ever afterwards regard himself as a seasoned campaigner.

John Kipling thought that the British displayed an almost morbid anxiety to be fair and to be seen to be fair in all their dealings with the native population. In order to do this, they had to show that they did not approve of British soldiers killing natives.[15]

Some years after the Kiplings had finally left India the 'gang-rape' of a Burmese woman occurred in Rangoon. The intention of the Governor was to hush the matter up, provided the offenders could be found and punished. The culprits were identified and court-martialled but, when brought before the court, the native witnesses, either through threat or bribery, refused to testify and the men were acquitted. When Lord Curzon, the Viceroy, learned about it he demanded that the accused be dismissed the Service and returned home. Not content with that, he had the whole regiment shipped off to Aden, (not the most salubrious of postings), its colonel sacked and the men's sergeant-major reduced to the ranks.

As well as the regular army there existed in Lahore a non-professional unit, the Punjab Volunteers. Its members attended regular drills and practised shooting at the butts behind the Lawrence Gardens. John Kipling deplored the tendency to make the Volunteers objects of ridicule, of the kind to which the Local Defence Volunteers were subjected at the commencement of the Second World War.

Apart from their military worth, Kipling felt the Volunteers played an excellent role by providing an enjoyable diversion for young men engaged in sedentary occupations: in his opinion the discipline was 'wholesome and salutory to the moral fibre,' which, he added, 'is apt to relax in these latitudes'. It was the duty of the Anglo-Indian community to encourage the force, especially as it was the means of 'uniting different castes of European blood.'[16]

In this respect Rudyard must have proved a bit of a disappointment to his father for although he had enlisted as a private in 'B' company, he failed to attend a single parade and had to return his capitation grant. Always filled with admiration for men of action, it seems he was not keen to join them, although the excuse that he lacked the time was probably a valid one.

During the month in which John made his plea on behalf of the Volunteers a contingent of the 72nd Highlanders, some Lancers, Sikhs and Punjab Pioneers passed through Lahore and John was moved to write in praise of the soldiers' wives, 'who take to gypsying with a good courage.' By gypsying he meant the slow work of jogging along in a little hut perched on a bullock-cart - travelling day after day at two miles an hour often accompanied by two or more children:[17] such was the lot of the Army's camp-followers. Not only did they suffer the monotony of seemingly endless journeys across that vast sub-continent, but also had to contend with the climatic conditions which prevailed in the Punjab where, in January, the temperature could fall to 40 degrees whilst, in June, it could rise well above a hundred in the shade: from July to September the humidity made things even more trying.

References Chapter Ten

1. KA 3/11
2. *Pioneer* 8.4.1870
3. *Something of Myself* p 57
4. *Pioneer* 9.5.1870
5. *Something of Myself* p.56
6. *Strange Ride of Rudyard Kipling* p.61
7. *Pioneer* 5.6.1876
8. *Pioneer* 21.2.1871
9. *Pioneer* 5.6.1876
10. *Pioneer* 15.7.1877
11. *Pioneer* 27.3.1877
12. *Pioneer* 5.12.1880
13. *Pioneer* 11.11.1877
14. *Pioneer* 13.2.1877
15. *Pioneer* 13.2.1881
16. *Pioneer* 22.11.1875
17. *Pioneer* 8.11.1875

7. Horse-dealers drawn by John Lockwood Kipling *(courtesy of the National Trust)*

The Ruled

For John Kipling one of the attractions of India lay in the fact that, like Shakespeare's Cleopatra, she was blessed with infinite variety. This quality appeared in her geography with its mighty mountain ranges, its great rivers, its huge desert, vast plains, forests and jungle. Ethnologically, she possessed more social groups, tribes, castes and races than any other land; as well as over 200 languages and dialects.

India's 'infinite variety' was found also in her fauna. She could offer a vast and varied animal population, both domestic and wild; the sacred cow, the despised pariah dog, the sacrificial goat, varieties of sheep; the camel and the water buffalo, the humped oxen, the stately elephant and the humble donkey. In her vast jungles and plains were to be found the tiger, the leopard, the cheetah, the wild boar, the wolf; monkeys and snakes too. In her mighty rivers, swarming with fish, were crocodiles - called by Indians 'muggers' and, erroneously by the Anglo-Indians, alligators.

It is not surprising that John Kipling's major literary accomplishment bore the title *Beast and Man in India*, nor that, when published in 1891, it proved to be an encyclopaedia of information comprising details of Indian customs, proverbs, superstitions, religion, folk-lore and dress. As in the case of the vast animal population, fact and fiction, habits and habitats, were all crowded together.

Was it true that, when allowed to stray, the camel automatically heads for Mecca? 'No,' replies Kipling, 'it has none of the homing faculty strongly developed in the horse'.[1] Is the Welsh legend of Gelert, the faithful hound, to be found in India? 'Yes,' replies Kipling 'in the Punjab there exists a tale which almost exactly parallels it'.

Rudyard loyally declared *Beast and Man* superior to anything he had written and there can be no doubt that he continually drew on his father's encyclopaedic knowledge as well as being, admittedly, in debt to John Kipling for some of his very best stories.[2]

John Kipling's early impressions of the Hindu people were favourable; he found them clever, amiable and easy-going, with a special talent for talking and writing but also with a great capacity for blundering.[3] Although he was to pronounce the Bombay servant the best in India, he found himself half-maddened by 'the curious lapses, the unaccountable forgetfulness and mysterious attacks of fatuity' to which he was liable. He accepted it as normal and justifiable for the European employer to hurl a boot at the 'punkah wallah' who fell asleep at his post and even, at times, to 'administer castigations'. When, after ten years of life in Bombay, the Kiplings moved to the Punjab, John complained that the Punjabi servant was 'wonderfully left-handed, clumsy and inept, not to say lazy'. He wrote: 'They serve us in the intervals of their abundant leisure,' whilst Alice complained that the 'everlasting now' had no meaning for them. 'There is a saying,' John added, 'that in every Lahore week there are seven holidays' and he went on to claim that 'neither Neapolitans, Parisians, Madrelinos nor Sheffield saw-grinders have such an appetite for loafing as your city-bred Punjabi.'[4] Indeed, he accused 'the servant problem' of being a source of marital discord. It was a regrettable facet of both Alice and John Kipling that they rarely, if ever, wrote about either the servants or the weather except to complain. In many ways both John and his wife were children of their age and shared its prejudices, especially with regard to the native inhabitants of India. There is no escaping the fact that at times they could both appear patronising and unsympathetic.

When John first encountered the Indian students who were to be his pupils in Bombay School of Art, he was not impressed: their capacity for indolence and slipshod work exasperated him. As he set himself to remedy these faults, he wrote: 'The Hindu aims at nothing and hits or misses by chance so that no one thing is quite right; no masonry is square, no railings straight, no road level.' He contrasted this slovenliness with the craftsmanship displayed in the P and O liners with their mahogany and brass fittings: in India, he complained 'one never sees a door that will shut, a latch that will catch, a stair-rail decently turned or a hinge decently fitted.'[5] When the generous Kutchi merchants offered to provide the opportunity for higher education for Indian children, John retorted that it would be 'much more worthwhile to teach a few to make a door fit, to build a decent boat and to plan a jetty for their tumble-down ports.'[6]

It was to such a task that he addressed himself, and not without success. Shortly after he left to take up a post in Lahore, the building of the new railway station was begun in Bombay and some of the delightful animal and bird carving on the stone-work was done to John Kipling's designs and executed by some of his former students. And when, at the end of the century, John was commissioned by Queen Victoria to supply designs for her new Durbar Room at Osborne House, he was able to commit the carrying out of the work to one of his Lahore pupils, Ram Singh.

Before he removed from Bombay, John had congratulated the native mounted police on the courage they displayed whilst bringing a run-away horse and gig under control. He also expressed his admiration of the way in which the police, both mounted and on foot, managed excitable crowds with coolness and composure. 'Just now', he wrote, 'the police as an institution are coming in for a considerable amount of abuse. It seems that clever young natives are alleging that torture, as a means of criminal investigation, had been introduced by the British whereas the truth was that it had long been recognised as an oriental procedure and strenuous efforts had been directed by the Chiefs of Police to put a stop to torture and intimidation.'[7]

A few months after he arrived in the Punjab John Kipling was to be found ruminating on the age-old problems of crime and punishment. 'We do not know how to punish crime,' he wrote in the *Pioneer*. 'What do these scoundrels care - they go to jail, get fat and are taught to read and to make carpets!' Then he recalled how, in the old days, punishment followed quickly on the offence and how the dacoit had his hands chopped off and was reduced to a crawling beggar for the rest of his life. He even recalled how one of his friends (described as 'one of the mildest and most amicable of men') looked back on former days with 'undisguised respect'. At the same time he admitted that the humanitarian mood which now governed in England made any return to those vindictive and cruel practices impossible, and that public hanging was now recognised as not worth preserving as a deterrent.[8]

When he came to study the native as 'a political animal',[9] John deplored the failure of the native citizens of Bombay to vote in the municipal elections: it was, in his opinion, a discouraging sign for those who had the welfare of Bombay at heart, not least for 'that large number of ardent and philanthropic persons of both sexes who had put on their bonnets and girded up their loins determined to raise the people of India to the level of a free and independent nation.'[10]

His conclusion was that it is almost as difficult to make ignorant, careless and corrupt men vote properly as it is to make unwilling horses drink. It would seem that, seventy years before the emergence of a free and independent India, John Kipling was pessimistic regarding its possibility. In his opinion the Hindus were unable to recognise that the solution to many of India's problems was bound up with the future of the Empire; nor did they appreciate all that the British were engaged in doing on their behalf, a view which was doubtless shared by the majority of the Anglo-Indian community at that time.

One class of Indian traders which Kipling eyed with tolerant amusement was that of the Pathan horse-dealers. He described them as 'lean of leg, smart and natty in dress, voluble in speech, with a lie and a straw forever in their mouths.' They reminded him of the horsey 'fraternity' he met in his childhood at the famous horse-fairs of Horncastle and Howden, whom the local gentlemen of the Kashmir Serai seem to match in all but the colour of their skin. 'The horse,' he wrote, 'like love, death or a bad cold, levels all ranks and assimilates the scamps, for whom he has a magnetic attraction, to a quaint uniformity of type.'[11]

The Kiplings were also concerned about the lack of humane feeling shown by the native population, even towards their own kind. Shortly after their arrival in Bombay, a pilgrim ship, the *Diamond* was wrecked half a mile off-shore. She was crowded with pilgrims bound for Jeddah but the local natives were content with the role of spectators, while half the European male population spent two days rescuing passengers and crew. On another occasion, John had reason to praise a British police officer, who dived several times, in an attempt to rescue a drowning Indian whilst his fellow Indians stood and grinned in scornful wonder, 'as they are apt to do'.[12] Again John described how a 'bheesti', or water-carrier, who had enjoyed something stronger than what he purveyed, fell down a well and was pulled out by an Englishman. His rescuer had proceeded to apply artificial respiration whilst the onlookers stared and jeered. This indifference regarding human life was extended to their European 'masters', so that when a friend of the Kiplings and his companion were left clinging to the mast of their capsized boat, the local fishermen refused to rescue them, until a reward equal to two months' wages for an Indian servant was guaranteed.[13]

Another aspect of Indian life which alarmed the Kiplings was the prevailing attitude to women, especially the child-bride and the young widow. John noted that elderly Brahmins showed a preference for very young girls and he quoted one of their sayings which ran: 'A man of sixty is like a young elephant; a woman at twenty is growing old.' His comment was that a man of sixty only resembled an elephant in size and, although poets were accustomed to write prettily about Indian maidens, 'there were no Hindu maidens in any strict sense.' He added: 'Millions of girls, bright and charming as any in the world, are deprived of that Spring-time of freedom and lightness of heart which is their birth-right.' Nor could it be, he claimed, that Indian girls reached physical maturity before Europeans.[14] He also protested against the practice of loading little girls with ornaments which sometimes led to their being murdered: 'irritamenta malorum', he called such jewelry.

The inevitable result of the yoking of a very young girl with a mature man was the proliferation of widows. According to the Puranic Code, to become a widow was the fruit of the wife's sins in a previous incarnation. Once widowed, even though only a child as young as three years, and with no experience of the realities of marriage, she was doomed to become the drudge of every member of her husband's family. Her hair was shorn and she was restricted to the inadequate diet of one meal a day. Without the death-bed permission of her husband, a second marriage was impossible. Even as late as 1925 the Swarajist politicians were denouncing the condition of child-widows as indescribable and in the eyes of the Mahatma himself it constituted a brutal crime.[15]

It was against this background that John reported on a double suicide which had occurred in Bombay. 'Mr Moroba Caroba,' he wrote: 'was a judge in small causes; he was also a Hindu reformer and, following his own principles, had married a young widow. As a result, he was so shunned by his caste-fellows that he and his bride, bound together, threw themselves down a well'. John explained: 'The girl went to her death richly dight in her gala dress and gold ornaments,' and added, 'Mr Caroba's zeal for reform outran his discretion and his marriage terminated even more tragically than ever its anathematizers dared to prophesy'.[16]

Not all the Indian people with whom John Kipling came in contact were ignorant, superstitious or poor. His very presence in Bombay was due to the wealth and benevolence of the race to which the city owed much of its prosperity; the Parsees. In 1865 the leading Parsee families were the Wadia, who built ships for the Royal Navy and the Tata who, though ruined when the American 'cotton bubble' burst at the end of the Civil War, had recovered and were well on their way to founding a new industrial empire. There was also the Jeejeebhoy family of merchants and bankers.

The founder of this great family, Jamsetjee, had been born in Bombay in 1783 and within forty years had become very rich. In accordance with the tenets of his religion, Zoroastrianism, he had engaged in a series of benefactions which included the building of a hospital, the endowment of several schools and, in 1855, the founding of the School of Art to which John Kipling came in 1865.

Jamsetjee Jeejeebhoy had been knighted by the Queen in 1842 and created a baronet a few years later. It was his wife's concern over the high mortality among Indians crossing from Bombay Island to the mainland that had prompted the building, at his own expense, of the causeway which linked the Island to the City. When in 1857 Queen Victoria made him a baronet, there was a public outcry in Britain. Thomas Love Peacock, the satirical poet, protested at the admission to 'the peculiar Christian institution of knighthood' of men of the Jewish race and of Parsees.

> Sir Moses, Sir Aaron, Sir Jamesetjeeramajee,
> Two stock-broking Jews and a shroffling Parsee,
> Have got on the armour of old chivalree
> And have hoisted the Red Cross instead of balls-three.

John Kipling, however, held the Parsees in high regard. He believed that they had done many good things in the way of ship-building, charities, army sutlering, education and shop-keeping, so it was impossible not to respect them. When Sir Henry Bartle Frere, Governor of Bombay in 1865, described the Parsees as 'the most extravagant, fraudulent and most abominable liars in India', John leapt to their defence: he described the accusation as 'grievously unkind' and, subsequently, was to refer to his patrons, the Jeejeebhoys, as 'that princely family'.

Despite his indebtedness to Parsee generosity and his appreciation of their good works, John could not resist what may seem to us a rather tasteless jibe: it concerned the Parsee hat. He described it as 'a shocking bad hat which fits nowhere, protects nothing and is apparently useful only to stick a bouquet in the hollow back part.'[17] [18] His criticism must have carried some weight with that community for, by the Edwardian age, the Parsees adopted the fashionable silk-hat!

He also noted that the Parsees, though keen on cricket, had no liking for horses, so you never met a Parsee jockey or horse-dealer. 'Yet they shine,' he said, 'on the cricket field, the bicycle and on the stage.' They seem to have taken their cricket with the seriousness it deserves, for they regarded their victory over the Second Eleven of HMS *Forte* as a real feather in their cap. 'Just fancy,' wrote Alice, 'a Parsee hat with a feather in it!' It was apparently the one symbol of his nationality the Parsee refused to part with (until the

109

advent of the Edwardian silk-hat). His hat represented to him the racial superiority of the Parsee over all other races whom he regarded as his inferiors.[19]

John found the Parsee ladies physically attractive and far more 'liberated' than their Hindu and Moslem counterparts; also better educated. Ever susceptible to feminine charm, it was a meeting with a Parsee lady which prompted John's romance in two chapters, *Inezilla*, with its account of 'wild delights, the more tranquil pleasures and the bitter sorrows of that far-off time'. He even envisaged the coming of the day when a Britisher might claim as a father-in-law a Parsee gentleman, 'with a name half-a-yard long and a purse still longer'. It was from his Parsee friends that Kipling learned an amusing story regarding the Duke of Wellington. During his service in India, His Grace had developed a taste for mangoes. Sir Jamsetjee had sent a gift of the same fruit to the Queen, packed in ice. Only two mangoes survived the passage and were served when the Duke was dining with Her Majesty. Seeing the mangoes, he exclaimed: 'Ah mangoes, good! very good!' and promptly consumed both the survivors before they could reach the royal lips!

Kipling's inveterate curiosity led him to attend a Shia passion-week service in which this particular Islamic sect celebrates the death of its founder Hussein. 'They do this,' John wrote, 'with a kind of Passion Play which illustrates the final scenes of Hussein's life and martyrdom.' The sobs and cries of the congregation, and the wild hoarse speech of the preacher, reminded him of a revival meeting in a Primitive Methodist Chapel in Lancashire and Yorkshire. This was especially marked when the preacher came down the steps of the pulpit to stride to and fro among the seated congregation, quivering with excitement and stirring it to tears with a wailing rhythmic rage of speech broken now and then with the cry 'Hai Hussein!'[20]

John had noted that the Moslem religion was 'full of ingenious compromises and transactions,' but he added that 'a more frank defiance of the laws, by which they profess themselves to be bound, was a characteristic of Christians who maintain Thee in word and defy Thee in deed... Moslem saints as well as Hindu sadhus show kindness to monkeys,' he wrote, 'and it is quite intelligible that their gambols should serve to amuse the large and languid leisure of professional holiness.'[21] There is an impression that John did not like the professional religious of any creed, despite the fact that he was the son of a parson!

There was one sector of Indian life which roused in Kipling the spirit of compassion; the Eurasians. In Lahore was an orphanage for the children of poor Europeans and those of mixed blood. 'They are bright and intelligent lads,' he wrote: 'not much given to fighting or the ruder diversions of English schoolboys, but gentle, biddable and polite'. He felt it a grievous pity that so few opportunities for them lay in the future, for most of them were destined to become fitters or railway workers of some kind and to believe that Queen Victoria ate only tinned food (for them the height of good living).[22]

There were parts of the Punjab where some of the inhabitants were accustomed to go about in 'a distressing state of nudity.' John's solution to this social problem was the making of a regulation which required that several yards of good cotton cloth should be disposed around the body of every naked fakir and coolie. In this way, 'not only would decency be promoted', he wrote, 'but the size of Manchester would be quickly trebled!'[23]

Another feature of life in the Punjab was the rifeness of rumour. 'The most vague and incorrect statements are accepted and repeated without thought', said John and recalled that in Amritsar this practice had led to 'a case of gallinacide'. Apparently, in order to preserve the jungle fowl, the authorities had imposed a close season with a fine of five rupees for each bird illegally killed. The native mind asked if a wild skinny bird is worth five rupees, how much more would a fine plump barn-yard fowl be taxed? At least one inhabitant decided to cut his losses: he slew the whole of his flock and made his family to sit up all night eating them - a pathetic incident, which throws light on one of the several causes which led to the Mutiny. In that case it was rumoured that the new cartridges issued to the sepoys were greased with both pig and cow fat, an affront to the Hindu, to whom the cow was sacred, and to the Moslem for whom the pig is unclean.

Not all of John's opinions of Indian people were critical or patronising. Like his son, there were those of whom he wrote with admiration: such a one was Miah Sultan. In his tribute to this man, John extolled both his public service and private worth. The deceased contractor had lost money through the good work he had put into the Garrison Church at Mean Mir, whilst engaged in the building of the new cantonment there. He had also been responsible for the new Lahore Railway Station which, according to John, was one of the finest examples of brick-work in the Punjab. 'Like Tom Bowling,' wrote John, 'he never from his word departed'. Not only was he a good and honest workman, he was philanthropic too: many Britishers, down on their luck, had been lodged free at his expense. 'A contractor who, though losing money never tries to dodge from under his engagements but goes steadfastly putting in the best work is a kind of phoenix rarely seen in this world; a man of hard earned wealth with so kind a heart as Miah Sultan is no less rare', was how Kipling summed up this Punjabi's life.[24]

One of the features in the Indian community which Kipling admired was their love of the theatre and their thespian gifts. They had been taught by some of the missionaries to call it Shaitan Khana, Satan's Hall, but this did not dampen their enthusiasm for it. 'Opera', he wrote, 'is indigenous to India'. He had attended a performance of the opera *Rustum and Sohrab*, the Persian hero who fought and killed giants. 'Posing comes easily to the Parsee and spouting is as natural to him as trading,' was John's comment. He felt that Parsee opera should become an interesting phase of Art by the cultivation of its own strengths rather than the imitation of European originals. He was impressed by the fund of patience possessed by the native audiences, 'who will sit through miles of dialogue and recitative and watch with tireless interest the unfolding of the slowest pageant.'[25] In Bombay there were six

111

Parsee dramatic companies but he doubted whether, like his own Wesleyan forebears, the Parsee elders really approved of this theatrical fervour.

As if to prove that there is nothing new under the sun, the Kiplings were full of complaints regarding the Indian postal system. Whilst living in Bombay, John complained about the cost of posting a letter to England but still more about the fact that 'letters, shot into the air, were never found again in the hand of a friend', and that even when posted to well-known postal towns, and legibly addressed, they tended to wander aimlessly in out-of-the-way places, finally returning to the sender, 'like bread upon the waters, after many days'. One of the popular excuses proffered for these delays was the necessity of burying one's father, thus, 'in a land where a man's parents die several times a year and each occasion requires the attendance of a son or a daughter to perform their obsequies, delayed letters were inevitable.'

When the Ambala Sweep, which was regarded as an institution, had to be abandoned because the postal workers could not keep their fingers out of envelopes bearing ten-rupee notes, John was more amused than indignant and suggested that those who regretted being robbed of the lottery should comfort themselves by the thought that in so doing they were keeping the soul of some Aryan brother free from sin.[26]

References Chapter Eleven

1. *Beast and Man in India* p.269
2. *Life's Handicap* Preface xiii
3. *Pioneer* 20.9.1870
4. *Pioneer* 27.3.1877
5. *Pioneer* 14.2.1877
6. *Pioneer* 1.8.1870
7. *Pioneer* 16.3.1875
8. *Pioneer* 1.5.1877
9. Aristotle Politics
10. *Pioneer* 29.7.1873
11. *Pioneer* 16.7.1882
12. *Pioneer* 23.1.1871
13. *Pioneer* 2.5.1870
14. *Beast and Man in India* p.228
15. *Young India* 5.8.1925
16. *Pioneer* 21.2.1871
17. *Pioneer* 2.9.1887
18. *Pioneer* 11.7.1880
19. *Pioneer* 13.8.1873
20. *Pioneer* 6.4.1871
21. *Beast and Man in India* p.57
22. *Pioneer* 24.7.1876
23. *Pioneer* 12.6.1877
24. *Pioneer* 27.3.1877
25. *Pioneer* 7.3.1871
26. *Pioneer* 23.12.1877

8. Trix Kipling on "Yorick" *(courtesy of Misses Helen and Betty Macdonald)*

The Square Re-forms

Eleven years after the family holiday at Littlehampton, Alice Kipling was anticipating the re-forming of what she liked to call 'the Family Square'.

For some time she had felt it would be good for John to have young life around him. He had become so absorbed in his affairs that he had ceased to be the conversationalist he once was and his wife felt that he needed the stimulation of young society: those bright young creatures would bring new life to him. Thus it transpired that in the Autumn of 1882 Rudyard arrived in Lahore from his school at Westward Ho.

His father had found for him the post of assistant editor of the *Civil and Military Gazette*, daughter paper of the *Pioneer*. At that time the *CMG* was actively engaged in losing money for its proprietors to the tune of £1,000 a year, a situation which the aspiring journalist was to view as a challenge. Rud's future wife, Carrie, was convinced that his withdrawal from school, without the opportunity of going up to Oxford or Cambridge, was the result of his parents' 'greed for gain.' If Alice had any ulterior motive, it was more likely to have been the welfare of her husband. The real reason was simple; John could not afford a university education for him: maintaining the two children at school in England had strained his finances, already under pressure through the need to maintain two residences in India. It would be cheaper if all the family were under one roof.

In 1881, when they had been established in Lahore for nearly six years, Alice had to confess that she and John knew what it really meant 'to feel the pinch'. It was on that account that she stayed in Lahore at the beginning of the hot season of 1881 and only went to the hill-station when John had his leave. She found life very dull with most of her women friends away; the only bright spot she could find was the weekly tennis party.

It was not only Rud whom parental poverty robbed of a university education: his sister, Trix, suffered the same experience. Her father had urged her to study hard at school with a view to becoming a governess as he would never be in a position to leave her much money. Trix made such progress at Notting Hill High School that the headmistress hoped that she might stay there for two more years and then proceed to Girton, thus bringing honour to the school. That Trix would have had a distinguished career at Cambridge is undoubted for she grew up to be intelligent and witty; Viceroy Lord Curzon (himself something of an intellectual) was reputed to have said that Mrs Fleming (as she became) was the one lady in India with whom he cared to converse.[1]

What was not understood by Trix and her brother was that their father had no idea as to whether or not there would be a pension when, inevitably, he had to retire. When he died, his assets were valued at less than £1,000.

Apart from the obstacle presented by relative poverty there is little sign that, while at Westward Ho, Rud revealed his future genius as a writer. Whilst his cousin at Harrow was winning prizes, all he could boast was a solitary prize for English Literature. His father wished that to his quickness and brightness Rudyard could bring application and at least one of his school reports led to a fatherly wigging. His mother complained that in Rud's long and numerous letters there were times when school never received so much as a mention. With characteristic understanding John recognised that his son was passing through the difficult waters of adolescence. The Pater's diagnosis was acccurate; when scarcely fifteen, and on a visit to Trix, still at Southsea, Rud first met Flo Garrard and fell victim to the agonies, hopes and despairs of young love. Two years later he considered that they were engaged. His father wrote; 'there is no help for that sort of thing once it is begun. He must learn by the long, slow and painful processes of experience'.[2]

Rudyard's Aunt Georgie had hopes that her nephew might become a doctor; possibly she had in mind the family regard for another Wesleyan minister's son, Dr Charles Radcliffe but, after attending a post-mortem examination, Rud decided that medicine was not for him.

There were already indications that the boy possessed exceptional talent in the field of literature. He edited and wrote most of the school magazine, *The United Services College Chronicle* and even went so far as to interest himself in the printing processes carried out in Bideford. He was fortunate in having Cormell Price for a headmaster who was not only an old friend of Alice's family, but also an outstanding teacher of English composition and précis. It was Price who encouraged the young Kipling to develop his gifts in this field. He gave him the run of his 'brown-bound, tobacco scented library'; there Rudyard was able to steep himself in both ancient and modern poetry and prose. Not content merely to read other people's work, Rudyard pelted his mother with poetry, some of which they had printed for private circulation under the title *Schoolboy Lyrics*. It has been suggested that this provoked his disgust, but even so he was proud to present a copy to the Misses Craik of Warwick Gardens before his return to India in 1882.

The recall to India came sooner than expected. Through his association and friendship with the proprietors of the *Pioneer*, John Kipling had found a berth for his son as assistant editor of the *CMG*. It was said that one of the owners, James Walker, paid Rud's salary for his first year. Diplomatically, the proprietors sent the editor, Stephen Wheeler, to England to interview his prospective colleague. Wheeler must have caught a strong whiff of nepotism behind this appointment but, being a wise man, he recognised it would be politic to fall in with the wishes of his employers. At the same time he seems to have determined that the young cub should learn the hard way (which he did). There were times when Rudyard found Wheeler 'very irritable and tetchy' and himself in great need of patience and forbearance, a situation on which caused his father to encourage him with the thought that he was 'training for heaven as well as for editorship'.

When Cormell Price told Rudyard that he was to leave school at the end of the Summer term of 1882, the arrangement was not altogether to his liking. Indeed, he was tempted to cable his father 'I have married a wife and therefore I cannot come'.[3] The lady in question was Flo Garrard, like Trix a paying-guest at Lorne Lodge, Southsea, to whom, whilst only fifteen years-of-age he had written:

> What comfort can I send you, Sweet,
> Save that Pain is; we know not why;
> Save that Pain lives and will not die.

During the Summer of 1881 he spent part of his vacation at Sorrell's Farm, Fittleworth, West Sussex and, whilst there, wrote in desperation to Miss Plowden asking her to search for a photograph of Flo and, if she found it, to post it to him as quickly as possible. He was plainly in the grip of his first serious love-affair.

Nor was Rud's reluctance to return to India entirely on account of Flo Garrard. There could well have been some curiosity regarding the Bohemian life led by his uncle, Edward Burne-Jones and his circle. This included Dante Gabriel Rossetti who was then living at 16 Cheyne Walk with Swinburne, as his lodger, and Fanny Cornforth (as she called herself), as his housekeeper, model and mistress. Rud's father feared a break-down 'on the moral side'. Certainly, Edith Macdonald was disturbed by the depths of passion the boy displayed concerning Flo. Apart from an involvement with Flo, there were really no grounds for anxiety. When Rud returned to England in 1889 he was disgusted by the hordes of prostitutes who haunted the Charing Cross area of London which he compared unfavourably with his *City of Dreadful Night*. Passionate he might be by nature, but there was a strong vein of fastidiousness or puritanism in his character.

Removal to India in 1882 would have meant not only parting with his friends, Dunsterville and McTurk but also from his cousins. These included Stan Baldwin, with whom he shared a holiday in the Epping Forest after his release from 'the House of Desolation' and, in whose company he got into various scrapes. He was especially close to the Burne-Jones children, Philip and Margaret. In later years he became a sort of father-confessor to Philip who, like his father, was shy and sensitive and ready to fall in love at any moment. Rudyard and Margaret corresponded with each other for years and addressed each other as Dear Wop; later it became 'Wop in Albion' and 'Wop in Asia'. He described her as 'unfairly pretty' but when she married an Oxford Don, John Mackail, a radical with socialistic tendencies, the correspondence ceased; a 'kid-gloved socialist' was the epithet applied to Mackail for even then the word 'socialism' was anathema to Rudyard Kipling.

Another of his cousins was Ambrose Poynter who had the misfortune to have inherited his father's temperament but not his talent: he became an architect, though not very successful, and when Rudyard took Bateman's, Ambo was employed on the conversion of the oasts into domestic accommodation. Ambrose, with his dreams unmatched by achievement, was the source of *The Finest Story in the World*. He was also Rud's best-man when he married Caroline Balestier.

At some time Rud had once promised to obey his parents wishes until he became of age and so it was, as a dutiful son, that he sailed for India and reached Lahore in October 1882.

There must have been times when he found things irksome and regretted his filial obedience. His mother immediately insisted on the removal of the masculine side-burns he had grown, though she allowed him to keep his moustache. He was irritated when his father insisted on referring to his salary as 'the boy's 'pocket money' and offered to pay his bills. It seemed to the son that his parents still regarded him as the child, from whom they had parted in Southsea eleven years before, and he complained that even the beloved Pater treated him like a twelve year old!

After helping his father in the Museum, Rud was re-introduced to his future taskmaster, Stephen Wheeler, whom Trix was to label 'the Amber Toad'. By the end of the year he was boasting to his Aunt Edith that, as Wheeler had fallen off his horse, the whole weight of responsibility for the *CMG* was resting on his shoulders, a somewhat boyish exaggeration as the printing process was in the hands of Chalmers, the Scots foreman. He also sent Miss Mary and Miss Georgina Craik a poem in a rather nostalgic vein regarding his lost youth. It was entitled *Song of an Outsider* and ran:

> By now the heron treads the wet
> Slush swamps of Goosey Pool,
> Now proses vex my Latin set,
> That first set upper school;
> E'en across the summer's end
> The call-bell's clangour floats
> Down to the weed-hung rock pools where
> The juniors sail their boats.
>
> For me no call-bell rings, alas
> For me no proses are,
> No lounging on the playground grass,
> No sails across the bar.
> The hot winds blow, the punkah leaps,
> Incessant to and fro,
> Ah, well for those most lucky chaps
> Who lark at Westward Ho!
>
> The Sunlight through the palm tree falls,
> Full on the white-washed roof,

And worse than any college calls
Are printers' calls for proof.
No wonder while the punkah flaps,
And hell-like hot winds blow
I envy those too-lucky chaps
Who work at Westward Ho.[4]

It could be expected that the boy would feel lonely during his first year back
home in India: his mother had gone to England to bring back her daughter;
his father was away on business, so, apart from the servants, he was the sole
occupant of a spacious bungalow of fourteen rooms. He sought and found
comfort in the companionship of his horse and passed the time schooling him
over jumps or driving him in a bamboo cart. He was now seventeen years-
of-age but looked twenty three or four. Like his father, all his life Rudyard
was haunted by an inner loneliness and just as John wrote of 'Lone Jacks
each perched on his own inaccessible island of loneliness', Rud wrote 'the
human soul is a very lonely thing and, when it is getting ready to go away,
hides itself in a misty border-land where the living may not follow'. It was a
theme which recurs in *Life's Handicap* and in *At the end of the Passage*, he
told a story of four young men who had no special regard for each other;
who squabbled whenever they met, yet ardently desired to meet - as men,
without water desire to drink. They were lonely folk who understood the
dread meaning of loneliness.'[5]

Early in December 1883 the s.s. *Ancona* docked at Bombay bringing home
Alice and her fifteen year-old daughter Trix. A few days later in Lahore the
Family Square was again complete.

The parents were prepared to find that they possessed a lovely daughter,
for Miss Plowden had kept them informed, but they were not prepared to
find that she 'o'er-topped them all with a "statuesque beauty"' and that she
possessed a radiance which brightened up the family home, 'like a Swan's
Incandescent'. She was also endowed with a fair share of her mother's wit.

Rud at once set about teaching her to ride; an absolute must for a young
Anglo-Indian lady. He found her an apt pupil with good hands and much
courage but. at times, a lack of concentration which made her brother sweat.
He wrote, almost rhapsodically, to his Aunt Edith describing her progress
with her hair blowing in the wind and colour in her cheeks. Her father had
bought her an Australian 'waler' with a long flowing tale and a mouth like
silk: she called him Brownie and Rud used to exercise him, no doubt to make
him shed some of the boisterous behaviour which Trix might have found
hard to control. Whether Rud was well qualified to act as riding instructor
is open to doubt - unless one qualifies for that responsibility by frequently
falling off!

In April 1884 Trix went down with 'Indian Fever', possibly Malaria, and,
for thirty six hours, she was very ill. As she was regarded as too young for
her first season at Simla, her mother took her to Dalhousie. The Pater went

too but, after ten days, he was summoned to attend the Viceroy at Simla to discuss plans for the forthcoming London Exhibition. With her father gone and her brother in Lahore, Trix dubbed Dalhousie 'Dullhouses'. She had an aptitude for this kind of description: once she described Oscar Wilde's lips as 'big brown slugs' and added that he seemed to be 'modelled in suet pudding'. Like her mother, she could be pretty 'waspish' when so inclined.

Back at Lahore, Rud caught some form of enteritis and, having been advised by one of the servants to dose himself with opium, arrived at the office in a state of intoxication. Once again Stephen Wheeler was absent from work; this time through a bad attack of opthalmia, so severe that it blinded him, and the assistant editor found himself working ten hours out of the twenty four.

During the same year 1884, Rud and his sister produced a book, *Echoes*, described by him as 'all parody work for which Trix shows a great facility, being her mother's daughter'. Their joint effort was adversely criticised by the November issue of the *Indian Review*, which described some of the work as vicious and 'cut 'em up most savagely'. When the reading public learned that they were 'vicious' they rushed to buy and sales leapt; grounds, no doubt, for what Stalky would have termed 'a gloat'. The Pater was brought in to produce the lithographic designs for the wrappers. He also did a bas-relief for *Hand in Hand* by a Mother and Daughter: this shows Trix reclining at Alice's feet as she sits with a book open on her knee. On either side stands a tree and in the distance a lake or bay. It is signed in the corner, JLK.

The year 1884 proved to be of considerable consequence in the lives of all the Kipling family.

John was to find himself in line for becoming a member of the Most Honourable Order of the Indian Empire; Alice, to the making of an aristocratic friend who admired both her wit and charm; Trix to meeting a young man who became one of her many admirers and twice proposed marriage to her, and Rudyard to find an influential appreciator of his early work and one who, in later years, proved himself a friend in need.

All these developments were connected with the arrival in India of the newly appointed Viceroy, the Right Honourable The Earl of Dufferin and Clandeboye (later the Marquis of Dufferin and Ava). Lord Dufferin was accompanied by his wife, Lady Hariot Dufferin; his daughters, the Lady Helen Blackwood and her sister, Rachel; his sons, Viscount Clandeboye and the Honourable Frederick Blackwood.

Prior to the coming of the Dufferin family the Kiplings had occupied a lowly place in the social strata but with the arrival of the new Viceroy, their social standing underwent a sea change. Many doors were opened to them; Government House, the Commander-in-Chief and the Lieutenant-Governor of the Punjab put them on their Free Lists, which meant they were admitted to dinners, balls and soirées at all these houses; a privilege which in its turn led to many more interesting invitations. When the Viceroy and his entourage moved to Simla for the summer months, His Excellency took to dropping in at the Kipling bungalow to enjoy John's conversation and to take tea with Alice, who fascinated him with her wit and charm. Naturally, jealous tongues began to wag and it was hinted that the Kiplings had insinuated themselves into the upper circles of Simla society although, according to Trix, their membership of the Amateur Dramatic Company (apparently an élite society) was proof that this was not the case. One of the most hurtful rumours spread about was that Rudyard, with his dark complexion, 'had a touch of the tarbrush' or 'was only eight annas in the rupee'. This last insinuation was manifestly ridiculous as, until their arrival in Bombay, about six months before he was born, it is doubtful if Alice had ever seen an Asian gentleman and, certainly, she had never known one.

In Simla the Kiplings met up with an old friend, Walter Roper Lawrence, now Secretary to the Viceroy with an office in the main and only street known as the Mall. Another friend was Howard Hensman, the Simla representative of the *Pioneer Mail*, to which journal John had contributed for fifteen years. Hensman was believed to be in the confidence of Lord Roberts, the Commander-in-Chief (Sir Frederick Roberts at the time), and it was from him that Rudyard heard the stories of exploits on the North-West Frontier, which found their way into some of his tales.

Certainly the year 1884 and the next four years were to prove formative in the life of all the Lockwood Kiplings, as they were known.

References Chapter Twelve

1. *The Strange Ride of Rudyard Kipling* - Angus Wilson p.110
2. KA 1/11
3. Luke 14: 20
4. *Song of an Outsider*
5. *Life's Handicap* p.130 and p.160. Without Benefit of Clergy and At the End of the Passage

Simla - An Absurd Place

When Lord Dufferin described Simla as 'an absurd place', he had not in mind its general appearance, odd as this was: its absurdity, in his eyes, lay in the idea of the capital of the Indian Empire 'hanging by its eye-lids to the side of a hill'. (John Kipling called it 'that topsy-turvey metropolis').

The little town was situated on the narrow saddle of one of the hundred mountainous ranges which run 'like the waves of a confused and troubled sea' at the foot of the Himalayas.[1] Its altitude ranged from about six thousand feet above sea-level to eight thousand; it possessed only one street called the Mall to which its residences, large and small, were connected by a series of winding paths through the pine trees, a situation which provoked the Vicereine, Lady Dufferin, to remark that to go anywhere in Simla one needed 'the wings of a dove'.

Simla was so remote that it was not until Lord Dalhousie, a former Governor-General, had linked it with Ambala by building a road (known as the Tonga Road) that it could be reached by wheeled vehicles. Even then, the journey from the rail-head at Ambala took between two and three days, depending on the weather and the traveller's powers of endurance. It was not until 1903 that a narrow-gauge line was built: prior to that date the traveller, on arrival at Umballa, (now Ambala) was faced with a hard journey of more than a hundred miles.

The unique character of Simla lay in the fact that, although it was but one of many 'hill stations', it had become the site of the Summer residence, not only of the Viceroy and his entourage, but also of the Commander-in-Chief of the Indian Army, the Lieutenant-Governor of the Punjab and the members of their respective staffs.

On this account Simla became the goal both of those who sought relief from the oppressive heat of the Plains and of promotion-hunters, place-seekers and the like so that, according to Walter Roper Lawrence, the Viceroy's Private Secretary, you could scarcely hear yourself speak, for 'the grinding of axes!'

To describe the general appearance of Simla as 'funny' could not be regarded as unfair because, apart from the chief residences like the Viceroy's Peterhof and the Commander-in-Chief's, Snowden, the generality of Europeans were housed in Swiss-chalet type cottages perched in every nook and cranny of the hills.

From the variety of addresses which headed the Kipling letters from Simla, it may be deduced that they rented a different chalet each year. Some letters are written from The Tendrils, others from Violet Hill, Victoria Cottage and North Bank. At least one of these cottages was described by Rudyard as 'a shanty', so that when he was offered the hospitality of Kelvin Grove, the home of James Walker, banker and proprietor of the *Pioneer*, he was delighted. It seems that the prospect of sharing a work-room, even with his beloved Pater, did not appeal to him. The gossips had spread the rumour that the Kiplings lived in 'the native bazaar out of which they crept stealthily into Society', but innuendoes of this kind were no more than examples of the jealousies fomented by the popularity the family came to enjoy 'in high places'.

One such place was the vice-regal lodge, known as Peterhof: it was rented by the government from the Maharajah of Simur and described as 'an uncomfortable shooting lodge' and, by Lady Dufferin as the smallest house she had ever lived in. Lord Robert Lytton must have shared these opinions, for, during his viceroyship, he chose another site where, in 1889, a hideous Summer-palace, variously described as in the Scots-Baronial style (Lord Birkenhead) or as Neo-Renaissance (Angus Wilson) was built.

Although Lady Dufferin found Peterhof small compared with her previous residences, it was still large enough for the entertainment of the two hundred and fifty guests invited to one or other of six occasions during the Simla season. They danced in the dining room to the music of the vice-regal band whilst, within the grounds, there was a flat-roofed tent in which to hold receptions and durbars: there was also a tennis court. Lady Dufferin preferred more intimate parties of some twenty five or so guests, in which John and Alice often found themselves included.

Travel between the various Simla homes was at first by horse, pony or jhampan, a kind of litter borne of four. This was later replaced by a crude form of rickshaw, while the possession of a Dykes rickshaw from Calcutta was regarded as 'a status symbol'.

In true English fashion both the Kipling parents made frequent references to the weather, usually to complain about it. In the Autumn of 1881 John wrote to Editha Plowden: 'You have seen wet days at Simla but never have you imagined anything so dismal, so suicide-inciting as these days of dreary rain and concentrated misery'.[2] Nor was John alone in his opinion. Lady Dufferin complained that when 'the little rains' came they were not like the genial showers of her native Ireland but 'a malignant down-pour which rattled on the roof and rustled through the air like the cataract at Lodore'. When in June 'the great rains' began they lasted for ten weeks, precipitated landslides, demolished roads and fractured gas-pipes.

Simla began to attain social eminence following the Mutiny of 1857. Wounded officers were sent there to recuperate and, not surprisingly, both matronly and maidenly hearts were stirred as they nursed the wounded heroes: Simla was on its way to acquiring the reputation of being 'fast'. As it takes all sorts to make a world Viceroy Robert Lytton found the Anglo-Indians there 'grievously good' and complained that members of his Council were accustomed to hold prayer-meetings in each other's houses, then depart and write scurrilous memoranda about their neighbours. When that famous

123

amorist, Wilfrid Scawen Blunt, visited Lord Lytton he detected in Simla an odd mixture of the conventional and the immoral, a conclusion confirmed by Edith Lytton who divided Simla society into 'the dowdy and the fast'.

Lord Dufferin told his Secretary, Walter Roper Lawrence, that nowhere in the capital cities in which he had served as British Ambassador had he found more delightful society than at Simla, and Lawrence described Simla society as numbering among its members some of the most refined, brightest and wittiest people he had ever known. Among those who contributed to this sparkling côterie were undoubtedly his friends, John and Alice Kipling.

Simla looked down on the hot dust-haze which hung over the plains below but there was one place in the district where these reminders of toilsome days and weary nights could not be seen; it was called Annandale and consisted of a man-made sports arena constructed through 'much levelling, much labour and much expense', according to Lady Dufferin. It was here that the sporting life of Simla, consisting of races, gymkhanas, polo, football and cricket, took place.

There was at least one occasion when young Rudyard entered for a four hundred yard scurry in the course of which the rider had to play on some musical instrument while riding a horse. His choice consisted of a tambourine fixed to the pommel of his saddle and beaten with the butt of his whip but where he came in the race received no mention! John travelled around on a pony but there is no suggestion that he ever engaged in the Annandale activities; rinking with roller-skating enthusiasts (especially the female) was more his line!

Annandale, reached by a steep descent through a forest of deodars, rhododendrons and ferns, was the brain-child of Lord William Beresford, Military Secretary to three Viceroys, Lord Ripon, Lord Dufferin and Lord Lansdowne and Master of Ceremonies in charge of both social and sporting occasions. He was also a hero who, following the Battle of Ulindi in 1879, had been awarded the Victoria Cross for the rescue of a trooper whose horse had been killed only a few hundred yards distant from 3,000 charging Zulu warriors.

According to Winston Churchill, William Beresford was not only a hero; he was a polished man of the world, a sort of Anglo-Indian Beau Nash and an accepted authority on matters of social etiquette and behaviour. In young Kipling he may well have seen a gauche and bumptious young 'news-hound', requiring to be 'taken down a peg or two': this he attempted to do.

The occasion was the Annandale Gymnkhana and the event known as the Victoria Cross Race, apparently based on the noble lord's heroic achievement. Each competitor was required first of all to construct a dummy, usually based on some comic figure such as the Indian ayah. He then had to race to the rescue of his creation over a series of obstacles and then back to the finishing line. Lord Beresford elected to 'rescue' a 'Special Correspondent'.

The Special Correspondent of the *Civil and Military Gazette* in Simla at the time was Mr Rudyard Kipling and apparently he was not amused. But he had his revenge in a story entitled *The Germ Destroyer*. The Pater always believed that the character of John Fennil Wonder was based on Lord William Beresford, described therein as 'a hard man with a soft manner and a morbid passion for work but whose officiousness had led Simla to agree that there was too much Wonder and too little Viceroy'; from this the good-natured Viceroy pondered 'if his dear, good Wonder had hired an assassin to clear *his* way to the throne.'[3]

If, indeed, Rudyard was guilty of using this tale as a means to revenge, years afterwards he made amends. In the opening chapter of his *Land and Sea Tales for Scouts and Guides*, he re-told the famous story of the exploit which earned Lord Beresford his VC; a little embroidered, no doubt, for the sake of his youthful readers.[4] But by that time Lord Beresford had been dead more than twenty years.

It was at Simla that the friendship between the Lockwood Kiplings and Lord Dufferin's family ripened. The Viceroy had come to India at a critical time and it seems that John Lockwood Kipling shared in the general perturbation among the Anglo-Indians which followed Lord Ripon's attempt to implement the Ilbert Bill. In 1885 he wrote to Miss Plowden that 'if Lord Dufferin had not come, poor Anglo-India would have gone crazy with vexation and apprehension but we have no end of confidence in the new man'.[5]

Lord Dufferin's approach to the problems of India coincided with those of John Lockwood Kipling. He warned 'intelligent, loyal, patriotic and well-meaning men of the dangers of applying to India democratic methods of government and the parliamentary system which England had only acquired through the discipline of centuries of preparation'. In the meantime he believed that repression, in the way of forbidding mass-meetings and incendiary speeches, was necessary. At the same time he recognised that the desire to share in the management of their domestic affairs was a legitimate and reasonable aspiration.[6]

Despite their political affinities, it is doubtful if Lord Dufferin and John Kipling ever saw eye to eye on matters relating to the Christian religion. John was an admitted cynic and unbeliever; the new Viceroy a product of Irish Protestantism with daily family prayers for his family and household and church twice each Sunday. The chief religious contribution Kipling Senior seems to have made to Simla were his designs for frescoes in the parish church.

Apart from this divergence of opinion, the cultured son of Eton and Oxford found he had quite a lot in common with the product of a Wesleyan Boarding School and a Staffordshire Art School. Both were blessed with a keen sense of humour; cultured, swift in repartee, good conversationalists; both possessed a keen artistic sensibility. Maybe, the very contrast in their social backgrounds added spice and interest to their acquaintance which was doubtless increased by John's possession of a witty and attractive wife.

Prior to her departure for India the new Vicereine, Lady Hariot Dufferin, had been asked by Queen Victoria to find out what could be done to ease the lot of the women of India, for she had been appalled by the stories she heard of their sufferings, not least during childbirth.

The royal request led to the founding of The Countess of Dufferin's Fund for the Supplying of Medical Aid to the Women of India: it was at Simla that the fund was launched. By means of it, British nurses and women doctors were encouraged to go to India and, eventually, medical schools for Indian women were established.

Years afterwards Lord and Lady Dufferin were travelling to South Africa aboard the *Kinfauns Castle*: one of their fellow passengers was Rudyard Kipling and, during that voyage, he presented Lady Hariot with a tribute to the service she had personally rendered to Indian women during the vice-regal years she had shared with her husband. It was entitled *Song of the Women*:

> By hands uplifted to the gods that heard not,
> By gifts that found no favour in their sight,
> By faces bent above the babe, that stirred not,
> By nameless horrors of the stifling night...
> Bid Earth be good, beneath, and Heaven above her.

His tribute may well have come at a time when it would be most appreciated for the Dufferins were on their way to visit the grave of their first-born son who had fallen during the Boer War.

Not so well received had been Rudyard's poem in celebration of the conclusion of Lord Dufferin's viceroyship. Entitled *One Viceroy Resigns* it embodied an imaginary conversation between him and Lord Lansdowne, his successor. Its scarcely veiled references (not always complimentary) to former members of the Viceroy's Council (including the Commander-in-Chief, Lord Roberts) had incurred the vice-regal displeasure.[7] Fortunately for Rudyard, Lord Dufferin was naturally magnanimous and, following Rud's breakdown, during his early years in London, His Lordship granted him the hospitality of his villa in Sorrento.

Rudyard's introduction to the Simla scene came during the first Summer season following his appointment to the *Civil and Military Gazette*. One of the proprietors, James Walker, who may have been responsible for his wages during his first year back in Lahore, gave the young man a month's holiday at his Simla residence, Kelvin Grove. He went there 'with the bottled-up energy of a year on his lips' and enjoyed a round of picnics, dances, theatricals and flirtations.

The next year Rudyard's report on the visit of Lord Ripon to the Maharajah of Patiala earned him the reward of being appointed Special Correspondent to the *CMG* for the 1885 Simla season. It was his boyish boast that it had cost him the loss of skin 'where a horse-man most needs it' for, in order to beat the Eurasian newsmen to the nearest telegraph office he had ridden thirty two miles in two and a half hours using two horses, having 'borrowed' the second one from a trooper in exchange for his own.

His first official season at Simla began somewhat inauspiciously with an attack of 'Lahore Sores', a disfiguring complaint about which the doctors seemed to have had little by way of a remedy. What aggravated the situation was the fact that the proprietors had urged on him the need to become a proficient waltzer. He had obediently applied himself to the mastery of this skill (something that he had always avoided), only to be mocked by the Pater who told him that the sight of his son revolving in the dance reminded him of the red bulls-eye of a lighthouse, a remark which cannot have added to the boy's self-confidence. It was not until six months had passed that Rud was able to report that his face was cured, even though he feared he was scarred for life.[8] The blemish does not seem to have spoilt his enjoyment of that first season for he was able to report that he had engaged in as much riding, waltzing, dining out and going to concerts in a single week as a life-time spent in Lahore could have provided.

The same year, 1885, gave Trix her first season at Simla. When she arrived it was shortly before her seventeenth birthday and, after the sheltered life she had led during her previous years, the social whirl of Simla, with its plethora of sophisticated 'grass-widows' and its crowd of elegant young men, resplendent in scarlet and gold, must have proved rather frightening to a young, inexperienced and innocent girl. The previous Summer she had been considered too young for Simla and sent up to Dalhousie (Dullhouses) where she had acquired the sobriquet of 'Rose-in-June'. In Simla she was to become known as the 'Ice-Maiden' by rejected suitors: but, in her early months, she found herself 'a wall-flower' and when asked by the kindly Viceroy why she was not dancing, she replied it was because she was only seventeen and by the time she was forty she would have some partners. Trix was too pessimistic (if she really made that reply) for by the end of the 1885 season her father wrote to Margaret Burne-Jones: 'Since Trix has been about I find myself much more popular with subalterns than I used to be. They didn't use to walk beside my pony for a mile at a time nor did they put on a propriety air, nor were they careful to slip in an occasional Sir. Mr Hodgson is one of a numerous host and he seems to be a very good boy but the nomination of this gentleman must not be taken to import anything.'[9]

The 'numerous host' came to include Lord Dufferin's eldest son, Viscount Clandeboye, who, if Trix in her 'declining years' is to be believed, proposed marriage to her both in 1885 and 1886. He had been newly commissioned in the 17th Lancers and when parental disapproval merged into concern the young man seems to have been conveniently 'posted' elsewhere. The supposed conversation of the Viceroy with Alice Kipling suggests that His Excellency first suggested that Trix should be removed to 'another hill-station', to which Alice Kipling replied with the suggestion that Viscount Clandeboye should be sent home. If, as his mother indicated in her memoirs, he was already commissioned, it is more likely that a posting was arranged for him, possibly to Dublin where the 9th Lancers were then stationed. In those caste-ridden days of Anglo-Indian society such a union would have certainly been regarded as a mésalliance, a fact which was no doubt appreciated by the Kiplings just as much as by Lord and Lady Dufferin. Years afterwards. and looking back on those Simla days, Trix reflected that at least she had been saved from becoming 'a widowed honorary Countess'. Had she and Clandeboye married, he would have taken the title of Earl of Ava when his father was raised to the Marquisate with the title of Dufferin and Ava. Unhappily, whilst serving with the 17th Lancers at Ladysmith, and appointed ADC to another of Trix's Simla partners, Ian Hamilton, Clandeboye fell mortally wounded at Waggon Hill.

Another of Trix's partners at Simla was the Queen's youngest son Arthur, Duke of Connaught.

After commanding a brigade of Guards at Tel el Kebir he arrived in India in company with his wife, Princess Louise of Prussia. We have it on the Queen's authority that the Duke came to know Mr Lockwood Kipling well.[10] One of the factors that drew John Kipling within the royal orbit was the Duke's interest in Indian brass-ware so that in 1884 Rud reported that his father had gone to Meerut to see the Duke about his collection:[11] He described His Grace as 'an affable old cuss' (he was thirty four) and added that the Princess 'could ride anything prettily'. Just as the Keeper of the Wonder House in *Kim* gave the Lama a seated Buddha in copper-gilt, an incense-holder and a pair of copper pots, so John gave the Duke of Connaught pieces out of his private collection.

It was this friendship between the Connaughts and the Kipling family which led to the designs for the billiards room at Bagshot Park, the Duke's country home, being made by John, also the carving on the legs of a full size table by the firm of Burroughs and Watts. The commission led to John Kipling being invited to make designs for the Queen's Durbar Room at Osborne House, although the actual work was done by Ram Singh, one of John's pupils.

Ram Singh's reward was a gold pencil and a signed portrait of the Queen. Princess Louise suggested that white and gold would be suitable colours for the Durbar Room, in contrast to the rather sombre Indian woods used at Bagshot. She also suggested that the new room should be electrically lit but the Queen disagreed.

Social life in Simla extended well beyond a round of dinners, dances and balls, and races: there was, for instance, Pellitti's coffee-house where people met to learn the latest bit of scandal or gossip. Whilst John Kipling loathed what he called 'the propagation of scandal', he found a bit of gossip more entertaining than the grim facts and obvious truths 'it was his habit to treat so ponderously'. It seems he did not take his journalism over-seriously!

All the Lockwood Kipling family were interested in the theatre. In the Pater's opinion the Lahore theatre represented the most intellectual and widely appreciated diversion the European community possessed. 'Like mercy', John observed, 'it pleaseth him who acts and those who look and listen'.[12]

When Rudyard came to play in such performances as *The Plot and the Passion*, he complained that a love scene - performing as they did in the Railway Theatre, Lahore - would be sure of interruption at a critical moment by a blast from an engine whistle!

The fact that all the family were invited to join the Simla Amateur Dramatic Company was proof to Trix that they had moved into the upper tier of Simla society. They performed in the pretty little New Gaiety where both the Viceroy and the Commander-in-Chief had private boxes. Lord Roberts also had the players perform at his residence, Snowden. There Rudyard played Brisemouche in *A Scrap of Paper*, the play which was first performed at the opening of the New Gaiety. He also wrote the prologue for a burlesque on *Lucia de Lammermoor* which was recited by Trix.

Like most Anglo-Indian mothers, Alice hoped that her daughter would 'make a good match'. The tastes in men of mother and daughter did not coincide. Alice complained that Trix never had any lovers; only men who wanted to marry her: Trix responded with the complaint that her mother always wanted her to ride or dance with men Alice preferred. Her parents noticed Trix's preference for older men as opposed to the youngsters who queued to write their names on her dance programme and even on her fan. Rud found the situation amusing, not least when Alice was ill with suspected diptheria (but which proved to be acute tonsilitis). She was nursed by Trix who had taken classes in home-nursing and ambulance work held by Mrs Ilbert; Rud's amusement arose from the sight of his sister 'applying poultices with one hand and handing off importunate lovers with the other'.[13]

Compared with her parents' encounter at Rudyard Lake, Trix found the first meeting with her future husband rather prosaic: they were introduced at a ball. After their second dance she thought she would be seeing much of this older man and noted that her reactions were quite different from those prompted by the young men whom Alice had encouraged (and Trix had found hard to get rid of); her intuition proved right: he called next day.

John Fleming, the object of Trix's interest, was a subaltern in the Queen's Own Borderers, but seconded to 'the Survey'. To Alice he seemed to be 'a model young man with all the virtues': in any case the fact that Trix seemed to find him acceptable must have relieved Alice from the fear that her daughter was becoming 'like Barbara Baxter who refused all the men until they axed her'. On the other hand John found the new man in his daughter's life austere and indifferent to so many of the interests which were dear to Trix's heart. To him John Fleming was the 'disturber of domestic peace, separator of companions and terminator of tranquility!'[14] Rud wrote to his friend Edmonia Hill saying: 'In these things I am no wiser than anyone else and I care for him (Fleming) ever so much'.[15] In Alice's opinion the best course was to let the lovers meet, get to know each other and then, perhaps, they would change their minds. John never came to approve of his son-in-law.

It may well have been that it was the domestic turmoil which her engagement to John Fleming provoked which led Trix to break it off. A year later John wrote to Editha Plowden to tell her that the lovers had 'knitted up the ravelled sleeve' shortly before he left Lahore to attend the Paris Exhibition. He expressed the hope that Trix had made the right choice but feared that she would discover Fleming 'thin pastures'; even though he was Scots, and 'a possessor of all the virtues': he was also ten years her senior. In the end Trix had her way and on her twenty fourth birthday, 18 June 1889, she went from the James Walker home, Kelvin Grove, to her wedding in Simla Parish Church. Her brother did not attend the wedding as he was already bound for England via the United States.

At the end of the Simla season of 1885 the family returned to Lahore, where Rud amused his father by falling in love. The object of his affections was a Miss Duke, the daughter of (in John's words) 'an awful military chaplain' who, he was told, 'preached impossible sermons,' but she reminded Rud of portraits of Emma Hamilton. By January 1886, when Lahore was experiencing the worst of the winter cold with rattling storms and bitter chill, his infatuation led him to undertake 'a chilly five mile drive, an absurd sermon, a cold church and a company of rifle-clanking soldiers, and about half a dozen other people', just to look upon the face of his beloved.[16] 'He really is funny about it', John wrote to Margaret Burne-Jones. However, disillusion was not far-off. Trix introduced her brother to the object of his worship: they danced together and he discovered the poor girl was suffering from halitosis. Her would-be suitor fled!

During his first season as Special Correspondent, Rud had engaged in a number of flirtations and his name had been linked with that of a Miss Parry-Lambert. But the association met with his mother's strong disapproval and she wrote, somewhat cruelly, 'Mrs Black's daughter is a dumpy girl... we thought her very plain until her cousin, Miss Parry-Lambert came and, by her transcending ugliness, made Miss Black seem almost beautiful'.[17] Like other mothers, Alice was inclined to turn a critical and perhaps jealous eye on any woman who threatened to come between her and her son. Little wonder that she came to view Caroline Starr Balestier with suspicion and declared: 'that woman is going to marry our Ruddy!'

The accuracy of her intuition was confirmed the following year. Rudyard returned to India for the last time with the object of spending Christmas of 1891 with his parents. It was whilst there he learned of the death of his friend, Wolcott Balestier; returned post-haste to England and, with his mother safely tucked away in Lahore, married the lady of his choice, Wolcott's sister, Carrie. In his youth he had been robbed of his side-whiskers; now he had become a man, he was determined not to be deprived of his girl.

References Chapter Thirteen

1. *Life of Lord Dufferin* - A.C. Lyall ii, p.103
2. KA 1/1
3. *Plain Tales from the Hills* p.128
4. *Land and Sea Tales for Scouts and Guides*
5. KA 1/11
6. *Life of Lord Dufferin* - A.C. Lyall ii, p.152
7. *Rudyard Kipling* - C.E. Carrington p.155
8. KA 1/10
9. KA 1/1
10. Diary 22.8.1890
11. KA 1/4
12. *Pioneer* 13.2.1881
13. KA 16/3
14. KA 1/11
15. KA 16/3
16. KA 1/11

9. The Gables, Tisbury, Wiltshire

Tisbury - The Square is Smitten

Carrie Kipling believed it was whilst staying with her and Rud at Brattleboro that John was persuaded to retire.[1]

The way to this decision had been prepared for him by the grant of a pension made by the government during Lord Lansdowne's viceroyship. No doubt Lord Dufferin had a hand in this concession as had also Walter Roper Lawrence, the Viceroy's Private Secretary. Lawrence's admiration and affection for John Kipling went back to his first posting to the Punjab where the older man had shown him exceptional kindness. Ten years later he was glad to use his influence to repay some of the many kindnesses he had received.

Nor was it only the prospect of a pension, and the persuasive powers of his son and daughter-in-law, that led John into retirement. Before the advent of air-conditioning and mepachrine, the Indian climate was not kind to Europeans. Lady Curzon, the wife of a later Viceroy, complained that India 'slowly but surely murders women'[2] and, although at one time Alice had been pronounced 'the healthiest woman in India', her health, like that of her husband, was being slowly undermined. When, in 1888, she suffered a severe attack of tonsilitis, at first feared to be the dreaded diptheria, it was attributed to 'a low condition'. A year later she was writing to report that John was suffering ill-health and how glad she was that their next journey home would be the last.

Many people were surprised that the Lockwood Kiplings chose Tisbury as the place of their retirement. Compared with Bombay and Lahore it seemed like a remote back-water. It was certainly remote but had the advantage of being on the railway.

A further attraction lay in the presence in the neighbourhood of Percy Wyndham and his family, friends of Edward Burne-Jones. The Wyndhams were also members of an upper-class côterie who called themselves 'The Souls'. The professed aims of this group were aesthetic and cultural pleasures and liberated morals, all of which must have had some appeal so far as John was concerned. The 'chief-priest' of this movement was Arthur Balfour, one of Burne-Jones' patrons and through whom he had first met the Wyndhams. Percy Wyndham had been Balfour's Private Secretary.

'Mr Kipperling', as the Wyndham children came to call him, became their drawing master (as he had done with Lord Dufferin's daughters) and, eventually, a close friend.

It was to be at Clouds, the great mansion where lived John's Wyndham friends, that he was to die, lovingly cared for by the family following the death of Alice a few weeks earlier. But he had some seventeen years of retirement to enjoy before, 'much broken in health and spirits', his body was carried to Tisbury churchyard to lie side by side with his wife under the east window. They had been married for almost forty six years.

The house in which John and Alice settled lay about a mile to the west of Tisbury; it was called The Gables and it may have been found through some Anglo-Indian acquaintance as it bears the same name as the Inn at Sippi Fair, five miles from Simla. Compared with the splendours of Clouds it was a very modest establishment consisting of a grey-stone house with red tiles and overlooking a cornfield. After her fourteen-roomed bungalow at Lahore, Alice found it 'a snail-shell of a house' and 'as crowded as a Persian omnibus'; and when John managed to smuggle new books into the already over-crowded rooms, the new-comers received a chilly reception from Alice.

Alongside the house was what Rudyard described as 'a tin-tabernacle'; this John thatched and there disposed his drawing portfolios, photo and architectural books and a hundred other 'don't touchems'.[3]

Clouds had been built to the designs of Philip Webb, another of the Burne-Jones' friends. It was in mid-Victorian gothic style and the interior decoration carried out by William Morris's firm: the paintings were by Burne-Jones. After having been destroyed by fire a few years earlier, it had been fully restored in 1893, the year that the Lockwood Kiplings came to Tisbury.

It was through the Wyndham connections that Alice and John were introduced to some of the other great houses including the residence of Arthur Morrison, a millionaire and the collector 'of all manner of beautiful things'.[4] Morrison was keen to enter Parliament and, whilst Rud was visiting his parents, he spoke at one of Morrison's political meetings. Also close at hand lay Wardour Castle, home of the Arundell family. The ruins of the fourteenth century castle, destroyed in the Civil War, stood in the grounds which had been landscaped by Capability Brown. The castle grounds became a place John Kipling frequently visited and where he was pleased to take his friends.

Another house where John was welcomed was the home of Lady Theodore Guest: it lay about nineteen miles from Tisbury. At one time her ladyship had hated the new-fangled motor-car and notices on her park gates read 'Motors not Admitted'. Eventually she became converted and sent her superb Daimler to fetch John who, after spending the August Bank Holiday weekend there, was 'returned home in style'.[5]

Frederic Macdonald believed that both the Lockwood Kiplings entered fully into the village life of Tisbury. He wrote: 'My sister became a court of reference to whom her neighbours made appeal... when for instance boys turned stubborn and daughters flighty. No one knew as much as she did about the mysteries of dress-making or the simple subtleties of cooking'.[6]

John, being a man who made all knowledge his province, became acquainted with gardeners, ploughmen, blacksmiths and farmers, learning from them and, according to Fred, teaching them too. Whether he took to English country-life as easily as Fred suggests is open to question. There were to be occasions when he complained about wearisome walks over farms and boring discussions about crops and live-stock. Other sources of ennui were house-parties and shooting parties which courtesy demanded he should attend but whose monotony, so far as he was concerned, was only relieved by the presence of 'pretty forms in gorgeous attire'.

It was to Tisbury that Rudyard took *Kim*, to be smoked over by his father and where 'under their united tobaccos it grew, like the Djinn released from the brass bottle and, the more we explored its possibilities, the more opulence of detail did we discover.'[7]

John had the novel idea of illustrating *Kim* by making low-relief plaques to be photographed in order to make illustrations.[8] A local school-boy was believed to have modelled for Kim whilst other villagers were persuaded to assume Eastern dress and model for the other characters in the story. It could be that in *The Woman of Shamlegh*; in *The Jat with the sick child*; in *Huree Babu* and *Mahbub Ali*, portraits of a by-gone generation of Tisbury villagers are preserved. What is more probable is that whilst they may have modelled for Mr Kipling, the faces were copied from the many drawings he had made of Indian heads during his sojourn there.

Whilst in Tisbury John was invited to present the prizes at the Salisbury Art School and to give an address. The prospect alarmed him but when a similar invitation came from his 'alma mater', the Stoke and Fenton Art School, he was delighted to accept. He was accustomed to lecture on India and manufactured lantern slides with which to illustrate his talk, fore-runners of the modern 'transparencies'.

As soon as John and Alice were settled in at The Gables it became the goal for family visitors. During the first year of his parents' residence there, Rudyard came from Vermont and stayed at Arundell House, Tisbury, which Alice had rented for him and his family. Edith Macdonald came almost before they were settled in and her brother Fred soon followed. During the following years several American friends, including the Doubledays, came and were duly taken to places like Wardour Castle, Fonthill and Clouds.

After five years of retirement, the shadows of bereavement began to fall across the home at Tisbury. Edward Burne-Jones died - dear Uncle Ned, whose country home across the Green at Rottingdean had so often opened its doors to John and his family. After cremation his ashes were interred beneath the west wall of St Margaret's Church. Rud was so grieved that he kept a two-hour vigil within the church.

At the turn of the year Rud had become so incensed by the pirating of his work by American publishers that he was determined to sail to New York and put a stop to it. Much against Alice's advice, he elected to take the three children, together with their mother and a nanny, with him. He had been doubtful about such a course but Carrie, who wished to visit her mother, insisted.

At the end of January, 1899, the family embarked at Liverpool on the RMS *Majestic*. The crossing of the Atlantic proved to be the worst in their experience: all the children were sea-sick and developed colds. On arrival they were met by their friends, Lockwood de Forest and his wife Julia but were forced to spend two hours in a draughty custom-house. Weakened by the sickness they had experienced during the voyage, the children developed whooping cough; Carrie and Rud had influenza which nearly lead to his death. While Carrie stayed at the Grenoble Hotel to nurse her husband, Julia de Forest took Josephine to her Long Island home where the child was attended by another American friend, Dr Conland. Unhappily Josephine, who had always suffered from digestive problems, died. On 6 March 1899, Carrie, who had neglected her diary during the dreadful weeks since their arrival, wrote: 'Josephine left us at 6.30 this morning'. Rud was still dangerously ill and it will never be known how Carrie eventually broke the tragic news to him; those who knew him well claimed that much of Rudyard died with Josephine.[9] After a short service in the de Forest home, conducted by the minister of Grace Church, Long Island, she was cremated at the Fresh Pond Crematorium. It is surely of some significance that in all his subsequent works, Rud made only two oblique references to his loss. One is in the poem *Merrow Down*; the other in a short story entitled *They*.

John Kipling's first reaction to the news of Josephine's death was to write to Carrie. 'I don't know what to say', he said, 'save that my heart bleeds for you and Rud in your sorrow. One of my comforts is you both have courage and still have each other and will, if possible, be drawn closer by the terrible bond of suffering and sorrow... I wonder sometimes, as one does helplessly, whether you have felt behind you any breath of sympathetic support from the great tides of feeling that your troubles have set in motion... I can't help feeling that all this weight of love may count for something'.[10] Alice wrote: 'Six little happy years: My heart is bursting full:'

John immediately prepared to sail for New York, where he arrived towards the end of March. His coming was greeted by their friend Sally Norton as the best possible medicine, bringing with him as he did 'his blessed English temperament, so steady and matter of fact.'

After Rud's convalescence, John arranged for them to travel with two friends, Frank Doubleday, who had been close by during the days of his illness and Edward Bok. Doubleday's friend Bok was the editor of the *Ladies Home Journal* which, according to John, catered for the taste of 'a refined feminine public'. Nor had he any idea that 'so much earnest endeavour, careful contrivance and high-toned sentiment' went into the paper's production. Bok described John as a witty and entertaining talker whose knowledge of Art and wide travel made him a rare conversationalist. 'When he was inclined to talk,' Bok added, 'he showed himself an encyclopaedia of knowledge, as extensive as it was accurate'.[11]

As the friends left Julia Catlin's home in Morristown, New Jersey the servant of their hostess, Mike, mistakenly packed Doubleday's trousers in John Kipling's luggage and vice versa. When he discovered the error, Doubleday dressed himself up in John's clothes. As he was exceedingly tall and John quite the opposite, the effect was ludicrous and made Rud laugh until the tears rolled down his face.[12]

Again, as the party sailed for England, Bok was thrilled to see one of the steerage passengers with a copy of his beloved journal. John's comment was that no such enlightenment was to be seen in the saloon! During the voyage Doubleday and Rud elected to teach poor Bok how to play poker, described by John as 'that capital game which I conclude is not a diversion for an honest man'.

John Kipling arrived back in England at the end of June to what he called 'Wiltshire greenness and a shrewd summer temperature of about 58 degrees - and, worst of all, work!' Mr and Mrs Doubleday accompanied him to The Gables which must have eased his return home. Rud and Carrie, however, found their return to The Elms more painful than they had anticipated. The house and garden were full of the lost child and Rud told Alice that he saw Josephine whenever a space was vacant at the table and 'coming out of every green dark corner of the garden, radiant and heartbreaking.' Carrie, who had hitherto been struck dumb by her loss, softened in the presence of Alice and broke down so that the two mothers 'had a long discourse, mingling their tears as women may and mothers must.' Alice had her own particular burden to bear. 'My heart is bursting full', she had written, 'both my children are so smitten'.[13] She was, of course, thinking, not only of Rud's most recent loss, but of the mental illness of his sister Trix.

The Flemings returned to India towards the end of 1890 and Trix soon found herself something of a star in the firmament of Anglo-Indian society. More beautiful than her mother, witty and intelligent, she enjoyed the admiration, among others, both of the Viceroy, Lord Curzon and the Commander-in-Chief, Lord Kitchener of Khartoum. Yet, within a few years she embarked on what were to become a series of mental breakdowns which compelled her return to England there to seek refuge with her parents at Tisbury. For the next twenty years mental instability was to overshadow her marriage and the declining years of her parents, John and Alice.

Rudyard laid the blame for this tragic state of affairs on those who, by encouraging his sister to involve herself in occult practices - the use of the Ouijah Board, the crystal ball, necromancy - were responsible for what he called 'the wreck of her mind'. And when, following the death of his son during the Battle of Loos, she tried to persuade him to get in touch with the boy's spirit, he responded with his poem, *En-dor* with its solemn warning, *And nothing has changed of the sorrow in store - For such as go down on the road to En-dor*. On the other hand, John Lockwood Kipling blamed John Fleming.

He had long disapproved the marriage on the grounds of incompatibility: in his opinion Trix and Fleming had too little in common: things which were of vital importance to her found him indifferent. John feared she might well find him 'thin pastures' and seek satisfaction elsewhere. In the end, whilst he was proved right regarding the unsuitability of the match, it is doubtful whether his reasons for so doing probed deep enough. The root causes of Trix's illness went back to her childhood and her marriage to John Fleming only acted as the catalyst which precipitated them.

The symptoms which characterised Trix's breakdowns consisted of long periods of stubborn silence which her mother called 'mutism'. These were often followed by incessant talk, most of it nonsense.[14] There were also violent hysterical outbursts in which she revealed a bitter revulsion towards her husband and which led her doctors to warn him against even visiting her in the nursing home where she was confined.

Much has been written about the psychological effects of the Southsea experience on Rudyard's later development. So far as Trix was concerned it would have been surprising if, when only two and a half, and apparently to her baby-mind, deserted by her parents, she had not suffered ill-effects. She was such a sensitive child that her aunt, Lady Poynter, had warned Alice to be careful with her as she was, 'more sensitive than any of us', whilst Rudyard declared that, compared with Trix, a tender plant was 'positively pachydermous'.

Again, as this sensitive girl moved into the stormy seas of adolescence, she lacked the guidance and support of her mother. Alice had declared herself anxious over 'the constitutional changes' her daughter was undergoing and Rud was troubled by the feelings of guilt Trix experienced, the product most likely of the dawning knowledge of her sexuality.

On her return to India and her introduction to the whirl of Anglo-Indian society, she preferred the company of older men to that of young subalterns. All the indications suggest that Trix was haunted by a sense of basic insecurity which had led her to seek, in Kensington, the consolations of religion and, in Simla, the company of mature men, eventually leading to her marriage to an austere, upright Scotsman, ten years her senior.

Marriage with John Fleming, rather than solving her problems, seems to have exacerbated them. In late Victorian times preparation for the physical aspects of marriage was practically unknown; thus most young brides went to the altar with little understanding of what the promises they were about to make entailed. In some cases the sole direction a girl might receive from her mother was on a par with 'just lie back and think of England'. A pall of prudery had enshrouded the British middle classes with the result that, although to enter the married state entailed child-bearing for possibly the next twenty years of her life, no truly 'genteel' girl was provided with much more than an inkling regarding 'the facts of life'. And the idea that a lady might find pleasure in the marital relationship was regarded as a slander on her sex. Nor could it be assumed that the bridegroom would be much better prepared. Such knowledge as he did possess would usually have come through whispers in the dormitory after lights-out, or from bawdy tales at the dinner party when the ladies had retired. Thus it is doubtful if this young Scots Presbyterian was much better informed sexually than his bride.

This being the case, and bearing in mind that Trix was burdened with a hyper-sensitive personality, it is understandable that after a few months of living together, she should embark on a series of breakdowns. Eight years after her first attack John, her father, remarked sadly that she was in better mental health when apart from her husband: could the 'Ice Maiden' of her Simla days have become the frigid wife of later years? It is true that, in between breakdowns, Trix entertained a warm affection for 'her Jack'; as she called him and to whom she stayed married to the end of his long life, though frequently they lived apart.

When Alice died just before Christmas 1910, her death precipitated another mental breakdown so that John was left to care for his daughter as well as to mourn his wife. He wrote to Editha Plowden: 'You have lost a friend who loved you - while I - but it cannot be written of!'[15]

Possibly aggravated by the years of constant tension and anxiety, Alice had developed an agonising form of neuritis although, according to Carrie Kipling's diaries, she died of Graves's Disease. John had already confessed to some form of heart-trouble which had condemned him to a dull life and no exertion; a few weeks after her death he followed Alice to the grave. Trix, on the other hand, lived to the age of eighty.

In the same year of Josephine's death, war came to South Africa and many of the Kiplings' friends were caught up in the conflict. Percy Wyndham's brother George was at Ladysmith with Trix's former friends, Ian Hamilton and Lord Dufferin's son, Clandeboye.

It was John Kipling's belief that Kruger had been preparing for war for years and that he was fighting, not for a republic but for a one-man dictatorship; described by John as 'a despotism feebly tempered by a corrupt and greedy obligarchy'. He summed up his views on the conflict 'since we have an Empire we must needs hold it'.[16]

Rud had presented his father with twenty five bound volumes of *Punch* dating from 1841 and John was struck by the comment they contained on the conduct of the Crimean War. 'They were word for word parallels to what we are saying now', he wrote. Following the disasters at Nicholson's Nek, the Modder River and Magersfontein (known as the Black Week of December 1899), John wrote: 'Our stupid army is demoralised by German brass-buttonism and parade-ground smartness whilst faced with a nation of intelligent marksmen who are led by skilled generals'. Although he believed we would emerge victorious, he also thought the war would only be won after much slaughter; but win we must if we were to exist as an Empire.[17] At the same time it was his opinion that, in accordance with tradition, the British Army had gone into the present war armed with the weapons and tactics of the last. He complained about the lack of proper training for the officers; 'fine fellows who will not take the trouble to learn their trade and who are content to be brave when they should be both brave and wise'. He was sorry that, owing to Trix's illness, he was unable to accompany Rud when he left for South Africa in February 1900 but looked forward to his son meeting Kitchener and 'holding colloquy with their old friend, Fred Roberts.' He took parental pride in the conviction that Rud's arrival 'would be worth much to our forces'; evidently he regarded his son as a war-winning factor.

Whilst John rejoiced in the publicity given to *The Absent-Minded Beggar*, he must have smiled when he heard of the snub administered to Mrs Moreton Frewen by the composer of the music, Sir Arthur Sullivan. Apparently Winston Churchill's sister-in-law pronounced the verses as vulgar, to which Sir Arthur replied 'And set to vulgar music too!' John dismissed J.W. Mackail's attitude to the war: in his opinion this consisted of lofty academic views which had little to do with reality; on the other hand, he seems to have found comfort in the English 'passion for fighting' which exceeded that of the Boers and the fact that the wounded had but one wish - to go back to fighting again; rare symptoms of jingoism, surely, in a mainly pacific character.[18] It is well known that when the war ended in 1902 there was nation-wide rejoicing. At least one exception was to be found in Rottingdean where Rudyard's 'beloved Aunt Georgie' hung out a banner on Northend House bearing the text 'We have killed and also taken possession'. Well-versed in Holy Scripture, the general public recognised that this quotation came from the Bible story of Naboth's Vineyard (1 Kings 21:19) and it was only Rudyard's intervention which saved Lady Burne-Jones from unfortunate consequences at the hands of a small mob, drunk on strong liquor and victory.

To employ Alice's words, 'the Family Square' had indeed been smitten but in 1904, at Rudyard's new home Bateman's, the old quartette was re-united briefly and, on sixth July of that year, joined in the celebration of John's birthday, the first time for many years.

References Chapter Fourteen

1. Diary 30.6.1893
2. *Curzon* - L. Mosley p.77
3. *Something of Myself* - Rudyard Kipling p.138
4. *Something of Myself* p.139
5. KA 1/4
6. *As a Tale that is Told* - F.W. Macdonald p.333
7. *Something of Myself* p.139
8. *Something of Myself* p.141
9. *Three Houses* - Angela Thirkell
10. KA 19/10
11. *Ladies Home Journal* June 1899
12. KA 1/9
13. KA 19/9
14. *Chambers Journal* March 1939
15. KA 19/9
16. KA 1/10
17. KA 1/9
18. KA 1/10

Best and Most Genial of Fathers

Shortly before Rudyard's twenty-second birthday he was transferred from the *Civil and Military Gazette* in Lahore to the parent paper, the *Pioneer Mail* at Allahabad. There he was made a special reporter and editor of the *Pioneer*'s weekly magazine supplement *The Week's News*. A few months later he was recalled to Lahore to take over the *CMG* editorship whilst Kay Robinson (who succeeded Stephen Wheeler) went on leave.

Rudyard wrote to Edmonia Hill: 'Lahore is not a nice place and I am lucky only in going back to the best and most genial of fathers, to smoke a pipe of sweet council with him.'[1]

The relationship which existed between John Lockwood Kipling and his son was a striking one, both in its depth and the fact that it endured throughout John's life. When he died, Rud wrote to his friend in Burwash, Colonel Feilden, 'My father was not only a mine of knowledge but a humorous, tolerant and expert fellow-craftsman... I do not remember the smallest friction in any detail of our lives. We delighted more in each other's society than in that of strangers... he was a Man and besides being all he was to me I'd worked with him for the better part of thirty years and he with me.'[2] The letter ended: 'So I felt a bit desolate' - probably this was something of an understatement.

The best description of John Lockwood Kipling by his son is found in the opening chapter of *Kim* where he appears as the kindly 'Keeper of the Wonder House'; the Lahore Museum. He is pictured there as a genial, kindly and learned man, well-versed in Buddhist literature. He recognised the Tibetan Lama as a fellow-scholar and treated him with respect and generosity, even to the extent of giving him a pair of his own spectacles. The Lama insisted on reciprocating by presenting the curator with a Chinese pen-case of ancient design and 'made of a type of iron no longer smelted'. Rudyard wrote: 'No wonder the collector's heart in the curator's bosom had gone out to it from the first!'[3] One suspects that the elder Kipling got the better of the bargain.

Out of his 'mound of books', 'the Keeper' had produced a huge volume of photographs and to the Lama's delight, showed him one of the lamasery from which he had come. He then proceeded to open a map on which they traced the places made holy for Buddhists through their associations with the Buddha's wanderings.

The whole picture presented is of a man, eager to do all in his power to help a simple holy-man whom he treated with the respect he deserved. When the Lama asked 'the Keeper' to indicate where the 'River of the Arrow', was to be found which cleansed those who bathed in it 'from every taint and

10. Rudyard Kipling with John Lockwood Kipling, The Pater, in 1883 *(courtesy of Misses Helen and Betty Macdonald)*

speckle of sin', 'the Keeper' replied, respectfully and rather sadly: 'Alas, I do not know - if I did I would cry it aloud.[4] He might have dismissed the whole idea contemptuously as the product of myth and legend (John, being by nature sceptical regarding all religions). But he refrained and thereby revealed himself as a sensitive, understanding character who was not prepared to trample on the dreams and spiritual yearnings of others.

In one of his later works, *Souvenirs of France*, written twenty years after *Kim*, Rudyard recalled that the Pater 'treated me always as a comrade and his severest orders were, at the most, suggestions or invitations.' Even so, when he arrived in Lahore to begin work on the *CMG*, Rud had resented the fact that his father seemed to treat him, not as a comrade but as a twelve year old; he had resented John's habit of referring to his salary as 'the boy's pocket money' and that he had offered to pay his bills. He had also been annoyed by the parental habit of referring to what John called his son's leanness' (he weighed eight stone five pounds). Rud preferred to think of himself as being 'in a hard condition!' Such pin pricks were no more than trifles and, in the first edition of *Black and White*, the son expressed his indebtedness to his father in mock-Elizabethan which, being translated, ran: 'If I have done ought of fair craft and reverential, it is all come from your hands'. A few years later, in his preface to *Life's Handicap*, he wrote that whilst only a few of the stories came from his father, 'these are the very best'.

Rudyard's admiration for his father was reciprocated and when in 1886 a new edition of *Departmental Ditties* was published it gave John great satisfaction, not least because the Viceroy, Lord Dufferin, a frequent visitor to his sketching room, professed to be struck by Rud's ability - 'To combine satire with grace and delicacy'.

A few years later, whilst staying with his son in London, John rejoiced in the fact that 'the Americans think more of him than the English and that's saying a lot'. He estimated that within the space of one year Rud had had more said about his work, and over a greater extent of Earth's surface, than some of the greatest English writers in their whole lives.[5] He admitted that this was in part due to the 'wholesale spread of journalism' but John's grounds for gratification were confirmed when one of Rud's fiercest critics, A.G. Gardiner, the distinguished Liberal journalist and essayist, admitted that Mr Kipling 'went up like a rocket out of the magic East and that his ascent constituted a dazzling spectacle'.[6] A few years later, when Rud visited Canada and successfully launched himself as a public speaker, his father was not surprised because 'on the Kipling side he was descended from three generations of public speakers; my father was, and my brother is, a really eloquent one.'[7] (He might have added that the Macdonalds were even more gifted.)

Whilst rejoicing in his son's literary success, John was glad that it did not seem to have gone to his head. Although as a young man he had been inclined to be 'bumptious', he was saved by his sense of humour.

During his early years in London he kept his head and had refused to be 'lionised', preferring to concentrate on his work. His social life was limited in the main to his cousins, Hugh and Ambo Poynter: John especially admired the latter for his commonsense and good manners.

He was not so sure about another of the cousins; Philip Burne-Jones. In John's opinion he was inclined to cultivate the superficial side of society - 'an arid and unsatisfactory diet' - but, in his unhappiness, turned more and more to Rud who, according to his father, 'had the noble gift of helpful comradeship and was a most kind and genial director for a discontented soul.'[8]

When John accompanied Rud on a visit to his old school at Westward Ho, he believed that his son derived more gratification from the half-holiday granted in his honour than a good book review.

It was not only literary guidance and encouragement Rudyard received from his father: he inherited several of John's characteristics, among them, a natural reticence. One of the striking features of John Kipling's journalistic work over a period of twenty years is the paucity of references to his main work; that of the Art Schools, first in Bombay and subsequently in Lahore where he was also Curator of the Museum. Apart from a few mentions of his activities, such as his plea that the Bombay school should not be relegated to the back of the city, and the occasional mention of the contents of the Lahore Museum, our knowledge of his daily work is limited to brief references made by other people who had occasion to visit him. In other words, self-advertisement was not a Kipling characteristic.[9]

One of the qualities which Editha Plowden found attractive in him was that, despite his encyclopaedic knowledge and accurate memory, he was not afraid to admit on occasion that he might have been mistaken. There was a combination of modesty and wisdom in the man which made him disclaim his fitness to be judge in his son's case on account of being 'too poor a judge' and 'too personally involved'.

Some of this modesty must have rubbed off on the young Rudyard for, in his earlier days, he confessed to his friend, Mrs Edmonia Hill, that he had a profound distrust in himself and found it hard to believe that he 'had a name for the making'.[10] His father, although doubtful regarding his own qualifications as a literary critic, had no fear of wounding Rudyard at the point where the creative artist is most sensitive - his work -for the boy never resented parental criticism. In consquence, John found himself always 'at liberty to speak and spare not'.[11]

When Rudyard viewed the prospect of his return to India with reluctance, his mother became anxious and fearful that if he remained in England he would be caught up in the fringes of Bohemian life. His father feared 'a breakdown on the moral side', presumably of a sexual nature.

There were certainly grounds for the parents' concern. Alice's sister, Edith Macdonald, had warned them of the intensity of Rud's passion for Flo Garrard and they were well aware of Edward Burne-Jones' amatory adventures and his friendship with the notorious Rossetti household at 16, Cheyne Walk.

Both father and son were conscious of the presence of a deep inner well of loneliness within them. John described this as 'the terrible individuality and isolation of the human spirit'.[12] In one of his letters to Miss Plowden he wrote 'We are all of us essentially alone' and described himself as being perched on his 'inaccessible island of loneliness.' In similar vein Rudyard wrote of 'the dread meaning of loneliness'.[13] There was much of the father in the son and of the son in the father.

As well as his son there were many who felt it a privilege to enjoy John's friendship: among them was Alice's brother, Frederic. Whilst he admitted that there existed 'important divergences of opinion' between them he recognised his brother-in-law's unselfish affection and general loveableness. 'The charm of his personality was felt by all,' he wrote; 'gentle, kindly, wise, everyone liked him and, of those who really knew him there was none who did not love him'.[14]

Eulogies of a similar kind can easily be multiplied and if John was still alive they would cetainly evoke his protests. He dreaded being regarded as a 'holy-holy' (should it not be holy-boly as in *Kim*?)[15] even though he looked like one'.

Many and varied tributes have been paid to his intellectual gifts, his wide reading, his encyclopaedic knowledge and his astonishing memory.

The famous scientist, Isaac Newton, is reputed to have said that if he had seen further than others it was because he had stood on the shoulders of giants: Rudyard would certainly have been ready to make a like admission for there is no doubt that much of the extensive knowledge of India found in his work originated in his father's erudition and shrewdness of insight, the fruit of his thirty years or so in that sub-continent. Not that John would even have dreamed of being regarded as omniscient but would have agreed with Rudyard when, in the preface to *Life's Handicap*, he wrote 'the Native and the English stare at each other helplessly across a great gulf of miscomprehension'.

Although remembered for his gentle tolerance, John was in some ways a rebel, especially when it came to the narrow moralism, the prudery and hypocrisy which so marred much that was excellent and robust in late Victorian Christianity. It is true that a portrait of that gentle, scholarly Wesleyan minister, his father, always hung in his study; yet he completely rejected, sometimes with surprising violence, the Faith of his Fathers.

In this respect John was 'a child of his age' for it was during the years of his adolescence that the first cracks had really begun to appear in the facade of traditional faith and morality. John was still in his 'teens' when George Eliot translated Feuerbach's *Essence of Christianity* in which the author denounced Christianity as the fruit of an illusion and a form of 'dominant subjectivity'. Six years later the much publicised debate on Charles Darwin's *Origin of Species* was held in the Oxford Union. Samuel Wilberforce, at the time Bishop of Oxford, spoke as the representative of Christian orthodoxy and was entirely discredited. Through these and similar events traditional faith was plunged into the melting pot and an age of doubt dawned.

It was not Christian dogma that provoked in John a delight in ridiculing the faith he had abandoned. Just as Edward Gibbon, born a hundred years before, had written about the religion of his forebears like one 'whom Christianity had seriously injured', so it was with John Kipling. Not only did he become a complete sceptic but took every opportunity to deride the religion in which he had been nurtured.

It was shortly after his arrival in Bombay that he arraigned 'the pernicious nonsense purveyed by the ecclesiastical wind-baggeries' who were accustomed to preach in the Cathedral; he confessed that after struggling to follow the preacher's commonplaces with half-closed eyes, he resigned himself to listening to sounds rather than sense. Many years later, when Alfred Baldwin, Stanley's father, suffered from depression and 'melancholia', John found it odd that 'piety and wealth and a loudly-asserted trust in a personal deity made people apprehensive and gloomy.'[16] On another occasion he referred disparagingly to the Baldwin residence at Wilden as 'a clanging, thundering home of all the virtues.'[17] Yet when Alfred Baldwin died in 1908 he wrote perceptively of 'the ease with which we bury other people's darlings'.

How did the iron enter his soul? It could not have been the product of his home background, characterised, as it always was, by the kindliness and tolerance of his parents. It could have arisen during his school-days at Woodhouse Grove where he suffered a mixture of sanctity and sadism: it might have arisen out of his experiences of Staffordshire Methodism when, in company with his employers and their family, he attended the local chapel. Whatever the cause, John never escaped a sense of something like regret for his lost faith. Thus when their friend Sibyll Heeley stayed with them at Tisbury, he envied her good fortune to have been born a Catholic and condemned in her the habit of continually examining and questioning her religion.[18] As with Thomas Hardy and the Dorset legend of the Oxen, so it was with John Kipling: despite all his doubts there remained the half of a broken hope that 'it might be so'.

A similar wistfulness was to appear in *Kim* when the Lama asked the curator 'Where is the River?'; meaning the River of the Arrow that cleanses all who bathe in it from every stain and speckle of sin.' The Fountain of Wisdom replied: 'Alas, my brother; I do not know!'[19]

In view of John's scepticism, merging as it did at times into antipathy towards the Christian Faith, it is rather odd that he came to enjoy the friendship of Lord Dufferin (a staunch representative of Irish Protestantism) and of Lord Roberts of Kandahar, the Commander-in-Chief in India. During the Boer War, Roberts had been so annoyed by the young Winston Churchill's adverse report of a sermon, given by one of Roberts' military chaplains, that for several months he refused so much as to speak to the writer.[20] It would seem that the charm of the Kipling personality prevailed where his opinions proved to be offensive.

Nor did age mellow him in this respect. Shortly after his retirement, in a letter to Miss Plowden, he described one of the bishops as 'long-haired, long-nosed and doubtless long-winded.' The visits of the local vicar's wife he found extremely tedious although he enjoyed a visit from the curate Charlie Hutchinson, 'always bright and cheery'.

He also appreciated the account given him by the vicar of an adjoining parish (with whom he had dined) of one of his flock who admitted that he 'had not spoke to his wife for more'n four year', the reason being that 'he didn't like to interrupt her'.

Life in India inevitably brought the Kiplings into contact with Christian missionaries; not surprisingly John showed scant regard for their effectiveness whether they were of the evangelical school, 'with the warm evangelical gush and the black-bound hymn book compiled from Wesley and Watts', or of their Anglican counter-part with 'the red-edged cross adorned prayer-book and monotonous Gregorian chants.'[21] When Miss Keene, the daughter of a missionary, won a gold bracelet at the Lahore Tennis Tournament, the Kiplings' household were not enthusiastic regarding her success. With so many of the Anglo-Indian community, they shared an aversion to missionaries.[22]

It is surprising to find that when the effectiveness of missionary work was denigrated by the Viceroy, (1872-76) Lord Northbrook, it was John Kipling who rose to its defence. The Viceroy had alleged that the missionaries' labours had so far wrought liittle change in the vast population of India, to which John replied: 'We are apt to undervalue the foundation for future action which has been laid by the devotion, learning and labour of missionaries'.[23]

Both in his private letters and his public journalism, John never sought to conceal the fact that he was susceptible to feminine charm: he frankly admitted that he found young and pretty ladies most attractive and, in his own mischievous fashion, took a delight in shocking his more straight-laced readers. His sly innuendos have led his literally-minded critics to believe that he was (in modern parlance) 'a dirty old man'. Certainly, there was something of the 'louche' in his writing but there was also a twinkle in his eye. He abhorred the prudery and false modesty with which many of his contemporary generation had surrounded anything to do with sex: he took a 'puckish' delight in shocking them and, whilst some of his readers enjoyed his sallies, there is no doubt that others were scandalized by them.

Despite John's admitted susceptibility to the opposite sex, there is no evidence whatever to indicate that he ever sinned in deed even though he admitted doing so in thought: though unrepentant he was always honest. He was certainly greatly attracted to Editha Plowden and on at least one occasion apologised, rather ruefully, for 'approaching too near the chalk line you have drawn'.[24] At the same time he admitted that, like a naughty boy, he didn't care. 'You are quite welcome to call the chess-board black or white as it pleases you or mark me down as an acquaintance or a friend at your pleasure. One doesn't change the nature of things by phrases, no matter how you turn 'em'.[25] For her part Editha referred to John, long after he was dead, as 'my kindest friend'. They corresponded with regularity for many years: she never married; maybe because although she had rejected what John, in a letter to her on 19 November 1909, called 'the new code of sexual manners and

147

morals' and which he attributed to G.B. Shaw, J.W. Mackail and H.G. Wells, it was to John Lockwood Kipling she had given her heart.

As for Alice Kipling, her family reputation of being a flirt was well-founded and the move to India did nothing to remove it. Her daughter accused her of having thoroughly enjoyed the passionate philanderings of her youth, so it is doubtful if they were entirely abandoned following her marriage. She admitted to enjoying the more permissive society of Simla, her favourite hill-station, and there is no doubt that the young men who walked beside her rickshaw wheels found this witty, intelligent and attractive woman most desirable. The possession of two grown-up children and a husband may also have endowed her with the added attraction of being 'safe'. What is certain is that, despite the temptations of Simla, the frequent separations which were part of their lot and the fluctuations of feeling which are part of most marriages, she and John remained devoted to each other to the end of their lives. Even in death they were not divided but lie side by side in Tisbury church-yard.

John Kipling frequently confessed to the sin of sloth; 'Work,' he wrote 'is an outrage; a vice of youth which I have long foresworn'.[26] On a number of other occasions he confessed to the sin of accidie and described himself as 'indolent and dilatory'. He wrote to Sally Norton: 'It's a cold world outside and the idle man has no place in it'.[27] Even his wife complained that, after his retirement, 'having nothing to do, he puts off doing anything' though, later, she was happy to report that 'after years of obstinate idleness John is at work again and is happier in consequence.'[28] It is certain that John would easily have admitted that he had often failed 'to fill the unforgiving minute with sixty seconds worth of distance run.' Perhaps it was another sign of his rebellion against the 'mores' of his forebears who believed not only in John Wesley's dictum 'Never be unemployed; never be triflingly employed' but, also in the proverbial saying, that 'the Devil finds use for idle hands'.

When the American invention called the stylograph came into his possession, he rejoiced in the discovery that it eased the physical effort of writing; unfortunately he accidentally trod on it!

A further weakness, to which this lovable, honest man confessed, was for his pipe. Because of it he became shaken by a persistent cough - a tobacco cough. He admitted it could be cured in a week by giving up smoking, 'which I haven't the pluck to do'. He even modelled a bas-relief plaque of himself complete with pipe at the base of which were inscribed the words 'Fumus Gloria Mundi'.

Rudyard shared his father's love of tobacco and, even when he was advised by his doctor to give up his pipe, he was either unable or indisposed to do so; but for that his life-span might have been prolonged.

Like all sensitive individuals, John Lockwood Kipling was quickly moved to compassion and his sympathies, with all forms of suffering, were easily aroused. Not only did he pity the extreme poverty and hardship endured by the rural poor; he visited the Grant Medical College in Bombay and, in the

Eye Hospital, was maddened by the sight of 'men and women, boys and girls, of all castes and tribes, slowly and helplessly losing their sight; dirt and ill nourishment being, in most cases, the prime cause.'[29]

Nor were his sympathies confined to the human species; he deplored the treatment handed out by Indian people to their animals: he even protested against the practice of confining wild creatures inside a zoo. In Lahore he sorrowed for Moti, the tiger, 'accustomed to traverse forty or fifty miles of territory in the wild state but now restricted to a few paces up and down his cage.' Surprisingly, for his generation, he deplored the Anglo-Indian passion for hunting and the importing of entire packs of hounds with which to hunt the jackal. None of these attitudes can have added to his popularity among the British community.

When each Spring was marked by the arrival of the troopships, *Malabar* and *Euphrates*, 'with their cargo of valour and beauty', he commented 'How lovely are the married ladies, fresh from the cool English air; fresh as primroses and daisies with a rose in the cheek'. He grieved to ponder how the climate and a succession of up-country stations would change all that.[30]

Again, standing with a group of mourners in a cemetery and hearing 'the beautiful words of the burial service', he wondered whether the thought that your grave would be as near as possible to England would prove any consolation during the closing months of your Eastern exile.[31]

Close to the cemetery stood the 'mad-house' and as he listened to 'the toneless, monotonous gibbering of the inmates', he wondered which death was less terrible; that of the body or that of the mind.

Both the Kipling parents were sensitive to the inevitable process of growing old. The sole occasion on which Miss Plowden remembered John being 'in a rage' was when his son wrote a sonnet in which he expressed surprise that his father was ever young and the parental response was: 'I was born with a bald white head and a round belly: the truth is I am only old in judgement and in understanding.' One of his letters to Miss Plowden concluded with the lines from the Hindi, 'I may be old; what then? Is my heart so old?' His sad conclusion was to the effect that 'old people should be resigned to their shelf, as long as they are comfortable and don't fall off' but such resignation eluded him.

The late nineteenth century Englishman usually had something of the 'male chauvinist' lurking within him; John Kipling was no exception. When, in 1870, Elizabeth Garrett received her medical degree from the Paris Medical School he wrote: 'The medical profession is to be opened to the ladies of England: why not the civil service of India? There are numbers of enthusiastic ladies who would be delighted to accept these appointments as the gentlemen of the educational service would be to welcome them.' He went on to imagine the accession of a number of 'solah (*sic*) helmeted Minervas, stern yet beautiful, admitted to the Olympian councils of the Empire'. 'India, he said, 'cannot lag behind the swift progress of the civilised globe!'[32]

Although he was a part-time journalist, John frequently made that profession the target of his wit. 'Journalism,' he wrote, 'is capable of many things; it divines the councils of kings and confidently prophesies the deep things of politics. Invention is occasionally called on to eke out halting knowledge (usually with happy effects). We all protest at these decorative treatments', he added, 'but they make the papers vastly more readable.'[33]

He recognised that the journalistic life is not always a happy one. 'Just when a piece of gossip that ought to be true is about to pass into history, it turns out to be baseless fiction, and the choice flowers of fun, for whose blooming in public report, one has patiently waited, die down to a stick not worth kindling'[34]

In a more serious mood he attacked the Press for 'blowing the bubble' reputation out of the dirtiest possible soap-suds.'[35] Echoing the poet John Milton he wrote: 'Earnestness and high moral purpose are out of fashion; the tide of corruption sweeps muddily past like the Indus in flood!' Evidently some residue of his puritan heritage still remained.

The wheel of rebellion against religious orthodoxy seemed to have come full circle when on Sunday, 19 July 1914 John Lockwood Kipling's grandson (also called John) was, of his own volition, baptised in St Peter's Church, Bournemouth, according to the rites of the Church of England. Both Rudyard and Carrie attended the service as sponsors: they left Bournemouth at three o'clock on the same afternoon and reached Bateman's in time for supper.[36]

About fourteen months afterwards, in the course of the Battle of Loos, the young man who might have continued his particular branch of the Kipling family made some 'unidentified corner of a foreign field forever England.'

Like Shakespeare's Prince of Denmark, the elements were so mixed in John Lockwood Kipling that a study of his life and works reveals him as a greatly gifted but very human person.

He was witty without being tedious; critical yet, on the whole, kind; a fountain of knowledge without being boring; he liked pretty women and never pretended not to.

A proud and affectionate father, he did not flinch from rebuking his son should he scent the presence of over-emphasis or a tendency to vulgar smartness.

On his own confession he was inclined to be dilatory and indolent yet proved himself a successful artist whether in clay or stone; with the pen, the pencil or the brush.

He was a distinguished master of design and a successful teacher, yet in spite of all these achievements he was content to live under the shadow of his famous son.

Small wonder that Rudyard Kipling considered himself blessed with 'the best and most genial of fathers'.

References Chapter Fifteen

1. KA 16/2
2. KA 15/2
3. *Kim* p.17
4. *Kim* p.14
5. KA 1/10
6. *Prophets, Priests and Kings* p.324
7. KA 1/9
8. KA 1/9
9. *Pioneer* 8.7.1873
10. KA 16/2
11. KA 1/11
12. KA 1/10
13. *Life's Handicap* p.161 - The End of the Passage
14. *As a Tale that is Told* - F. Macdonald p.339
15. *Kim* p.296
16. KA 1/9
17. KA 1/10
18. KA 1/10
19. *Kim* p.14
20. *My Early Life* - W.S. Churchill
21. *Pioneer* 2.5.1870
22. KA 1/10
23. *Pioneer* 22.7.1876
24. KA 1/11
25. KA 1/11
26. KA 1/9
27. KA 1/9
28. KA 1/9
29. *Pioneer* 3.10.1870
30. *Pioneer* 14.2.1871
31. *Pioneer* 12.9.1870
32. *Pioneer* 4.7.1870
33. *Pioneer* 26.6.1876
34. *Pioneer* 28.3.1871
35. *Pioneer* 10.7.1876
36. Mrs Kipling's Diaries - 19.7.1914

11. The Ruby Prince drawn by John Lockwood Kipling *(courtesy of Misses Helen and Betty Macdonald)*

12.   The Snake Woman drawn by John Lockwood Kipling *(courtesy of Misses Helen and Betty Macdonald)*

Subject Index

159